Semper Fi

Teren Fzj

FIDELIS

FIDELIS

A Memoir

TERESA FAZIO

Potomac Books

AN IMPRINT OF THE UNIVERSITY OF NEBRASKA PRESS

Acknowledgments for the use of copyrighted material
appear on page 215, which constitutes an extension of
the copyright page.

Library of Congress Cataloging-in-Publication Data
Names: Fazio, Teresa, author.
Title: Fidelis: a memoir / Teresa Fazio.
Description: [Lincoln]: Potomac Books, an imprint of
the University of Nebraska Press, [2020]
Identifiers: LCCN 2020007564
ISBN 9781640123557 (hardback)
ISBN 9781640124004 (epub)
ISBN 9781640124011 (mobi)
ISBN 9781640124028 (pdf)
Subjects: LCSH: Fazio, Teresa. | Iraq War, 2003–2011—
Personal narratives, American. | United States. Marine
Corps—Officers—Biography. | Women marines—
Biography. | Women and the military—United States.
Classification: LCC DS79.766.F39 A3 2020 |
DDC 956.7044/34092 [B]—dc23
LC record available at https://lccn.loc.gov/2020007564

Set in Minion Pro by Mikala R. Kolander.

For my family, and for those Marines who felt like family

Contents

Acknowledgments

There are so many people without whom this book would not have come to fruition. For their commentary on early manuscript drafts, I would like to thank April Darcy, Adam Dalva, Brian Castner, Georgia Pollak, Marissa Unger, and Phil Klay, as well as incredibly supportive writing instructors Kerry Cohen, Sue Shapiro, Kara Krauze, Matt Gallagher, Mark Slouka, Peter Trachtenberg, Askold Melnyczuk, and Susan Cheever. I am grateful for not only Tracy Crow's editing advice, but her crucial introduction to Potomac Books. I also appreciated early feedback from the students and instructors at the NYU Veterans' Writing Workshop, Voices from War, Words after War, and the Bennington Writing Seminars. Many thanks to Jim Dao at the *New York Times* for taking a chance on my first article, which inspired this entire project, and to the Corporation of Yaddo, which awarded me a residency at a crucial point in this book's journey. Thanks also to Tom Swanson of Potomac Books for seeing potential in *Fidelis*, and to his colleagues Leif Milliken, Rosemary Sekora, Emily Wendell, Elizabeth Zaleski, and Patty Beutler for helping this book come to life.

Humble thanks and Semper Fi to the Marines I knew on active duty and while deployed, especially those whose experiences are incorporated here. I was privileged to work alongside incredible people. For my tribe of dear friends and family, both civilian and military, who witnessed me living this story and then writing about it (and sometimes about them)—thank you for all you have said, done, and held over the past sixteen years. Your efforts to listen, empathize, and offer support have been invaluable. I would like to extend thanks and compassion to my mother, father, and stepfather, and deep thanks to Mike, Chris, and Josh: the best brothers in the world. Finally, heartfelt thanks to Boyan, who may not even know how much he's stoked my courage.

Author's Note

Names and certain identifying details have been changed. Conversations and quotes have been reconstructed from memory to the best of my ability.

FIDELIS

Prologue

I sleep four hours on the tailgate of a roofless Humvee. My watch alarm beeps as the battalion lurches into activity. We load up, slam the armored doors, and trundle off in convoy. Before daybreak, we cross the line of departure. A spray-painted cardboard sign points an arrow: Iraq. Fuck. I'm in Iraq. I'm holding a rifle. A loaded pistol's strapped to my jacket. Fuck. I think of Ms. Hopper, my old band director, the chest-high striped pants, my glinting clarinet. College physics exams nearly flunked despite fancy ROTC-financed schooling. Lot of good that does against roadside bombs. My clumsy midshipman antics, spilling brass polish on the first day of indoctrination. Fuck. I am an idiot. What would my high-school math teacher say to this? He taught me trigonometry on the back of a pizza box. And for what? So I could be a rolling target for anyone hiding under the bridges of this cloverleaf? The cosine of 2π is—fuck. We crash through a pothole, and my gut leaps through my gullet. Really? My last thoughts might be freshman-year math problems? I should be having deep, profound insights if I could die any minute. Instead I'm hungry. How many calories are in the jalapeno cheese spread? Short palm trees line a path in the distance. I keep my weapon pointed outboard, fingers straight and off the trigger, safety on. Small children sprint from a mud hut to greet us, precious collateral damage. The sun rises in an overcast sky. My A-Driver tears open a bag of Skittles, yawns, rattles them into his mouth. He seems unconcerned. He was here last summer.

ONE

Packing for War

Camp Pendleton, California

A month and a half earlier, when I checked into Communications Company, Camp Pendleton's breezes carried mown grass, salt air, and the paint-and-industrial-cleaner aroma of decades-old warehouses. Gold "butterbars" shone on my green service dress uniform, along with sharpshooter rifle and expert pistol badges, and a yellow-and-red national service ribbon—the "pizza stain." My shiny oxfords clicked from the asphalt parking lot onto a cement breezeway; the company office's thin brown carpet lay beyond a glass door. I took a deep breath and went in.

Captain Davis, Comm Company's second in command, offered an immediate handshake; he was just then assembling the list of troops who'd deploy. "Welcome aboard! Wanna go to Iraq?" he said, all sandy buzz-cut and laughing brown eyes.

"Do I have a choice?" I asked.

"Put her on the roster!" he shouted, grinning at the other Marines. We'd leave in four weeks.

My mom's gonna kill me, I thought. But there was no reason for me not to go; we'd been at war nearly a year. I'd seen the "shock and awe" airstrikes on TV from a bland Quantico cubicle, where I'd worked for six months while waiting for Communications/Information Systems Officer Course. Toward the end of our training, our instructors had warned us we'd probably deploy immediately.

Within the month, Captain Davis baptized me "Little T." At twenty-three years old, I stood five foot one: the youngest and shortest officer in the battalion. Short hair and glasses dialed down my scarce femininity, while pixilated camouflage hung loose on my small frame. The combined effect was less *Hurt Locker* than *Harry Potter Goes to War.* Potbellied Chief Warrant Officer Clive, whose mustache twitched when he talked, teased I'd started kindergarten the year he'd gone to boot camp.

Soon I sat at a folding table in front of a laptop, which the enlisted Marines joked was an officer's "standard-issue weapon." Sometimes my Ethernet cable blinked green, and the internet worked; sometimes it didn't. I wasn't assigned to a platoon or in charge of any troops yet; in the scramble to leave, Captain Davis would figure out a precise assignment for me later. I didn't know it then, but broken wires—this bane of communications troops—would dog me over the next eight months.

Within the next few weeks, I drew a Kevlar helmet and a flak vest one size too big. I fitted the straps on my pack, pulling them ever tighter; supply ordered me an extra-small pair of steel-toed boots. Mercifully my issued gas mask worked well when I, Clive, and thirty-odd others filed into the gas chamber. Though an armory clerk issued me a pistol, there was no time for the shooting range. Instead I stood in an hours-long line for shots against yellow fever, typhoid, anthrax, and smallpox, the last of which gave me swollen glands and chills. I sealed the pus-weeping vaccination site under a waterproof bandage, sweating out fever on my roommate's couch. It would take a month for the scar to form.

When I told my roommate Nell that I was deploying, her curly hair bounced with excitement. She'd returned from Kuwait a few months before, where she'd helped dismantle a base from the initial invasion. Petite and athletic, the second youngest of seven children, she'd saved my sanity back at the Basic School, telling corny jokes as we'd dressed for early-morning hikes. Her sunny disposition had survived Quantico's gas chamber, where she'd brought a disposable camera, thinking our red-eyed choking would be hilarious to preserve on film. Whether she was training for a marathon, dancing at a club, or rolling down the Pacific Coast Highway with an open sunroof and Pink tunes blaring, her enthusiasm was contagious. Over the next few weekends, we savored frozen yogurt and In-N-Out burgers while I shopped to go to war.

I blew a hundred bucks at Walmart to stuff a coffin-sized footlocker with shampoo, detergent, Ziploc bags, and candy. At Staples I spent an embarrassing $385—one-sixth of a bimonthly paycheck—to individually laminate every page of my *Communications/Information Systems Officer Course Field Book*. It nestled in the footlocker along with a foamy blue pillow, a Christmas present from one of my three younger brothers. I added a deck of cards and a box of stationery I'd had since middle school. A month later, unlatching the box in Iraq, I'd discover M&Ms that tasted like soap and the bar mitzvah invitation from a former classmate.

This deployment was partial payment of my Reserve Officers' Training Corps debt; in exchange for full tuition and a stipend, I owed the Marines at least four years of active duty. Packing for war marked the culmination of four years of study, eighteen months of training, and fifteen years of running far away from home.

I stuffed fear way down in my rucksack, tucking resentment of my divorced parents between tight folds. I scrunched in homesickness for my brothers, pushed away insecurity over the college boys who'd rejected me, and stripped down deployment's discomfort along with the bed linens. I counted out T-shirts and shorts, and folded new desert camouflage into duffel bags inked with my last name. Their seams puckered in silent rebuke. A laptop case held my new Dell. Inside I tucked extra underwear, one clean T-shirt, and three more bags of M&Ms.

I slid my will into a green L.L. Bean backpack, the kind with a reflective stripe. If I died, my brothers would split my savings account, my mother would get my college ring, and my uncle would get my sword. On a sheet of notebook paper, I scrawled funeral instructions for a Roman Catholic ceremony, a couple of schmaltzy song titles, and to be buried with the pink blankets I'd slept with since birth. Deployment would be the longest stretch I'd sleep without them.

By the time the alarm went off on my final morning in California, I'd burst awake with adrenaline several times. In the last minute before leaving, after I'd switched off my cell phone and secured my shiny medals into a Strawberry Shortcake lunchbox, I grabbed a blue bag I'd lugged around since summer camp. In went the folded blankets. I buried my face in them, inhaling deeply their comforting scent. My scent. Then I zipped up the bag.

Our other two roommates in California had deployed within the previous few days, so that morning, Nell drove me to the mustering area at Camp Pendleton. Palm trees stood at attention while chubby toddlers gripped their camouflaged fathers' necks. Wives cried. A master sergeant growled, "My kids don't need to see this shit." He'd bid his family good-bye at their house. As I threw my seabags onto the pile, dawn gave way to bright chill, and my nose and cheeks reddened. Someone snapped a group photo of a few other lieutenants, a chief warrant officer, and me.

In the photo I look wary, awakened too early, my mouth set in a hybrid of resignation and feigned cheer, arms tense at my sides, my camouflage blouse bulging over a new leather holster laced with stiff rawhide. By the time I get to Iraq, I will have traded the shoulder holster for a smaller one on my hip, and the cast of characters in the photo will have come to life.

On the parade deck, families stood aside as Marines assembled a formation, confirming social security numbers and blood types. We filed into white government buses for the trip to March Air Force Base. Asphalt whizzed by under the windows, and I drowsed until bumps in the road jerked me awake. Within a few hours we clambered up metal steps onto the 747, weapons in hand. We wouldn't need ammo till later.

We officers flew business class. I sat next to Marla, Comm Company's only other female lieutenant. Red-haired and lithe, with a drop-holster strapped to her thigh, she had started one class ahead of me at the Basic School and Communications Officer Course, and had joined our unit eight months prior. She peered at me with concern as we buckled our seat belts; she'd grown up the second eldest of four girls. I looked away, shrugging out of my holster and missing my brothers. After wheels-up, she pushed her seat back, stretched long, slender legs, and read a paperback novel. We traded mystery thrillers and romance novels for the next fourteen hours. The flight attendants, proud to have Marines aboard, passed an American flag down the aisle for us to sign. They brought as many Kit Kats and pizzas as we could stomach. It felt strange to be feted in this way, like a calf gorging before slaughter.

A few hours in, a steward cast his shadow over my tray. "I didn't realize we had two *princesses* on board!" he said, bending toward Marla and me. "Where you ladies from?"

"You gotta be fucking kidding me," I growled. I hated anyone who singled us out from the males. I was a warrior. Princesses didn't join the Marines. But Marla offered him her name, rank, and our occupational specialty: communications. The flight attendant brought us toiletry kits, with toothbrushes, toothpaste, an eye mask, thin socks, and moisturizer. He didn't bring them to anyone else. I dubbed mine "the princess kit," shoved the toothbrush and toothpaste into my briefcase, and left the eye mask and socks in the seat pocket in front of me. Within minutes, Marla had slathered moisturizer on her hands, reclined bootless with her new lounge socks on, and adjusted her eye mask for a nap. I kept my eyes open for the next round of snacks, fidgeting in my new desert trousers, already a little tight.

After eighteen hours, around midnight, we landed in the dark of Kuwait City International Airport. The air smelled alien and stale. During our bus ride to Camp Victory, our temporary Kuwaiti camp, I couldn't see anything.

We waited at the camp, the size of several city blocks, for orders to convoy north. Days stretched into a week, then two. To combat the late-February chill, I wore issued brown poly-propylene long johns under my uniform.

There wasn't much room for physical training, and Camp Victory's sand proved too soft to get in a proper run. Once or twice, I tried jogging around the camp's perimeter, dodg-ing ropes and stakes holding the tents up every ten feet. After-ward I dumped sand from my sneakers. The next day I woke at 0530 and crept to the small gym tent in the dark. The "gym" had rubberized mats on the floor, a rickety recumbent exercise bike, and a silent television tuned to Bangladeshi MTV. I ped-aled slowly, half-awake, the taste of toothpaste lingering in my mouth. The badminton-themed Bollywood video made me feel only farther from home.

No flush toilets graced Camp Victory; instead, Porta-Johns baked in the sun. They steamed with excrement and urinal puck and sexual frustration, doors inked with Sharpied pussy. By way of laundry, I took socks, underwear, and T-shirts into the shower with me, rubbed soap on them, and hung them to dry over a cord that Marla and I stretched over our cots in a seventy-woman tent. When the water tanks ran low, I crouched naked under a trickle of cold water in the shower trailer.

Though I craved solitude, we Comm Company officers trav-eled in a herd. Nervous I wouldn't fit in, I stuck close to my com-rades to ensure I frittered my time acceptably. Captain Davis and the other male officers opened their tent to wage multiday cribbage campaigns. Marla, the staff noncommissioned officers ("staff NCOs") and I passed around the "Iraqi Most Wanted" card deck. In their mug shots, most Al-Qaeda and Ba'athists scowled. But Sultan Hashim Ahmad Al-Tai, the eight of hearts, grinned so wide as to set me giggling. Even when we weren't playing cards, Marla only needed to say "eight of hearts" to make me laugh.

Manning a laptop mp3 playlist, I cued a Guns N' Roses cover of "Cat's in the Cradle," but as the opening chords strained, the captain said, "Turn it off. Reminds me of my boys." Two blond toddlers awaited him back home. Several other fathers chimed in, "Switch the song." Many had been part of the initial invasion the previous year, and they'd spent only four months home between deployments. My fingers flicked the touchpad to Dynamite Hack's "Boys in the Hood." After that, I picked only fast songs.

Since I didn't yet have a platoon of my own, Captain Davis assigned me temporary supervision of three technical control Marines. TechCon was the heart of the communications network we'd set up in Iraq, a nexus of routing, switching, and multiplexing gear. Sergeants nicknamed A-Ville and B-Ville were a study in contrasts. Blue-eyed, serious A-Ville had majored in math at an elite East Coast college and kept his hair as shaggy as Marines were allowed to get. Balding and goofy B-Ville had secretly embarked a unicycle into the TechCon equipment van. Both called their fair, freckled staff sergeant "Shark," playing off the hippie first name, Ocean, with which his parents had graced him. All three troops were brilliant.

Since their TechCon equipment was en route to Iraq in embark containers, A-Ville, B-Ville, and Shark's Kuwaiti responsibilities involved mainly video games, and they invited me to play *Jeopardy!* one morning. I clambered through the dark, mostly empty tent to a metal folding chair, while they perched the laptop on something mostly stable: a chair, cot, or plywood table. These were the few furnishings available on all of Camp Victory. For the first and last time in my Marine Corps career, my high-school academic team triumphs came in handy, and I crushed them. They couldn't have known that I'd been banned from academic team practice one day a week to give others a fair shake at questions, or that my brother Zach had ceased trivia games with the blunt words, "this is not fun." When A-Ville, B-Ville, and Shark rewarded me with unswerving loyalty, I felt blessed to have drawn such a nerdy occupational specialty as communications.

In Comm Company, the chow line marked a thrice-daily social hour. We turned our bodies to block the wind, squinting as the line crept forward. I nodded along with debates over the recent Super Bowl, whether the Kuwaiti laundry could be trusted to return one's clothes, the business model of the guy selling $5 camel rides, and rumors of when we might convoy into Iraq. I never volunteered my own opinions, wary of falling afoul of the crowd's consensus. The chow trailer's entrance bore pink liquid soap above two slop sinks, and when paper towels ran out, we dried our hands on our trousers. Breakfasts included yogurt, white bread, and powdered eggs. Lunches and dinners comprised meat stews, soft vegetables, potatoes, and rice. We shuffled our cardboard trays down the line and staked out round stools at cafeteria tables. I rotated my seat from left to right, in constant motion, still not used to this sea of new people.

One night at dinner, Jack took the seat across from mine. He was tall and broad-shouldered, with olive skin, and his dark hairline receded over an intense brow. Red-and-black bars pinned his collar: Chief Warrant Officer 3.

We locked eyes over our trays of meat and rice. The chow hall's clatter stopped, and I quit fidgeting. I hunched over my dinner and looked away.

Jack asked my military occupational specialty.

"Comm," I said. "You?"

"Nuclear, biological, and chemical warfare, but now I do mortuary affairs."

"Oh." We were in the same battalion, but I said nothing more.

"The decontamination stuff is similar," he said, papering over my awkward silence. When he smiled, his dimples puckered. His eyes shone a marbled green. I looked down again.

"Do you have a family?" he asked.

I cocked my head. Didn't everyone have at least part of a

family? "Two brothers and a half brother, two stepbrothers and a stepsister, mom, dad, stepmom, stepdad," I said, cataloguing my complex family with a little belligerent pride. As I chewed a bland forkful of rice, I realized most other officers had spouses and children of their own.

"Uh, do you have a family?" I asked, a beat late.

"What's left of it," Jack muttered. Now it was his turn to look at his meal.

"Oh. Sorry," I said. *Shit, is his wife dead?*

"A really great kid," he said. "He's seven."

Oh my god, she's dead and I'm an asshole. "My youngest brother is seven!" I said. We spent the next fifteen minutes comparing notes on our respective favorite second-graders. My half brother Zach had ocean-gray eyes and loved swimming. I'd visited his class in dress blues before I deployed. Jack took his son, Sebastian, sailing and helped him assemble Lego robots. He'd been teaching him to field a baseball before deployment. During the following afternoon's cribbage game, Jack loomed over my shoulder and peeked at my cards, his forehead grazing my temple.

After three weeks in Kuwait, we learned of our impending convoy: one day to get to the border, two days to get to our base ten miles west of Fallujah. The rumor mill swirled, manufacturing certainty that IEDs littered our route. The Sunday before we left, I attended my first Mass in a year.

The priest entered the chapel tent wearing a white cassock, singing, *be not afraid, I go before you always.* He knew half of us would soon rumble away in Humvees. I squirmed in my plastic chair; camouflaged bodies walled me in. My throat constricted, and I wanted to bawl; I glimpsed a few other stricken faces. I fingered a tissue, bowed my head, and angled my eyelashes so tears gathered on their tips. Pretending to blow my nose, I wiped them away.

Don't be a pussy, I thought. I swallowed my spit the same way I used to when Mom told my brothers and me to go fuck ourselves, or when Dad harangued us about her leaving him, or when our stepdad screamed at us if we didn't ask permission before touching the TV or fridge. When the hymn ended, my throat opened and tears subsided. The chaplain blessed us, two fingers and a thumb held high.

TWO

Convoy

Camp Victory, Kuwait

On the morning of our convoy from Kuwait to Iraq, we saddled up in Humvees, a row of armored hulks against the moonscape. The M16 rifle slung over my shoulder reached below my knees. My pistol sat on the front of my flak jacket in a green nylon holster, its handgrip facing my right side, easily accessible should I need to shoot anyone at close range. The Marines had spent the previous night bolting on vehicles' bulletproof doors, Mad Max versions of gear we should have already been issued. Even so, our Humvee had no roof. As my driver fiddled with the radio, checking comms, he joked Uncle Sam had loaned us a slick convertible. My cargo pockets bulged with field-stripped MREs: my favorite wheat snack bread, a pouch of peanut butter, a sleeve of mashed potatoes I'd only eat if I got desperate. As we waited for word to leave, the troops squabbled over snacks. Charms hard candies meant bad luck, my A-Driver explained, hucking a pack of them into the desert. After one last head call, I dolloped hand sanitizer into my palms, ready to go.

Engines coughed to life, and we rode out in a column of dust. As we turned onto the highway, I felt jittery, though I knew this was only Kuwait. Nothing interrupted the flat white-sand horizon.

We arrived late the first night at Camp Navstar, a supply contractors' base just before the Iraqi border. An advantageous location, I guessed, for the Marines to stay up late fixing vehicles. Stumbling back from the head, I ran into Jack and was surprised he recognized me in the dark. He'd spent the past several hours on the side of the road with a broken-down truck, helping the mechanics patch it together. The truck clanked and spewed oil smoke; it wouldn't top thirty-five miles per hour, but at least it was running. I said I was glad they'd made it—if barely—and wished him good night.

I curled up, a sleeping-bagged larva, on my Humvee's tailgate, a place where only someone my size could fit. Four hours later, I woke to my watch-beep with a thumping pulse. I found a Porta-John, swigged water, chewed MRE bread, and refilled my CamelBak. In the cold dark, as tires crunched gravel, we crossed the border.

Morning wore on as we rumbled north from Basra. I buckled my seat belt—might help, couldn't hurt—and pointed my rifle where the window should have been. The cheap foam donut under my helmet kept it perched high enough so dry wind chapped my nose and cheeks. Beside us, miles of desert unrolled: mounds of dirt, a patch of distant green, and once, a tent punctuating the monotony. A shepherd strolled alongside his flock, wielding a reedy staff, far enough away that we paid each other little mind. In the more populated areas, smooth concrete houses stood patched with cement, their walls' chipping paint revealing intricate blue and green patterns. Elderly men waved cupped hands, beauty queen gestures from figures in wrinkled tunics and billowy pants. We called their *dishdashas* "man-jammies." An elementary-aged boy and girl hailed us from their dirt driveway, their family's skeletal tractor parked a few yards away. The cars near these houses—small white trucks and sedans from the '80s and '90s—looked as if they still might operate. Maybe. Farther along the highway stood lopsided mud huts with tilted windows and iffy roofs, if they had roofs at all.

Here, between Basra and Nasiriyah, "Uncle Sam's slick convertible" suddenly didn't seem so sketchy.

I'd expected the graffiti-scarred Arabic road signs, but the additional English translations surprised me, until I remembered Iraq's former colonial status as a British mandate. I would love to say now that in that moment, I soberly contemplated my own unit's status as yet another occupier of Iraq. But it wasn't the way I was thinking. Deployment marked my first journey outside the United States since a single high-school band trip to Montreal. When I dreamt about travel as a teenager, I hadn't envisioned packing heat.

Sunburnt by the afternoon, I wiped my sweaty palms on my trousers; the wisps of clouds did nothing to block the blazing sun. I fished a camera from my cargo pocket and aimed a few touristy snapshots, keeping one hand on my rifle, immortalizing its front sight post in each photo's foreground. I'd meticulously pecked the grid coordinates of our way stations into my GPS, a Christmas gift from my father. The U.S. model didn't carry Iraqi maps, but I could see the line we'd traveled. There was only one road, and everything else was sand. I tracked how far we'd gone, yelled it up to the driver in case he was interested. He wasn't.

We stopped for a ten-minute security break. A long line of waiting cars snaked by; they'd been stalled behind our lumbering convoy. A white Toyota sedan slowly passed. Two men, bearded and burly, sat up front. Three women cradling children were crammed into the backseat. One mom looked out the window; she wore a black hijab, but no veil. Her eyes, full of worry, scanned our column of armed Marines. In her lap sat a squirmy kindergarten-age girl, sucking her thumb. I didn't know where they were coming from, how long they had to go, or what awaited them at the end of their drive. As the car evened with my position, the mother's eyes stopped at me and deepened; in my baggy uniform, I must have looked twelve years old. I lowered my rifle, smiled, and gave her a small wave. She saw I was female. Her face crinkled into a smile; both mother and daughter waved. I felt connected, awash in pride.

I will admit now that I thought the Iraqis might love us, callow as that may sound. I thought maybe I was making a difference, showing them what a woman could do.

What a woman could not do, however, was pee in public without baring ass. The stark desert landscape stretched unforgivingly open, and our next ten-minute stop marked my only chance for a head call. I wrangled my nylon belt and unclipped the gas mask pouch strapped to my left leg. To avoid exposing my untanned rear to every Marine in sight, I opened both doors on one side of the Humvee, making a stall. Then I ordered my A-Driver to turn around in front of me and stand guard. My driver faced away from the other side of the vehicle. I peed as fast as possible, jiggled my legs a little to drip-dry, and rebuttoned with a quickness.

Our convoy resumed crawling forward. Soon more children appeared along the roadside, none cradled by parents. When we slowed, they scampered up near our vehicles: first one kid, then two, then four, then a swarm. Marines threw Skittles, one-liter water bottles, and MRE packets, all against the rules of engagement. Two kids, age seven or so, tried for my attention, rubbing their bellies in the universal sign for "hungry" and pressing their palms together in supplication. My response was similar to how I dealt with panhandlers at Grand Central: shake my head, avert my eyes, keep moving. But children very rarely beg in the United States. These two had soulful-puppy eyes I was ashamed to meet. Watching them made me feel complicit in their poverty. Feeding children seemed like a fundamentally human mission, a plausible reason for us being there.

When I was a child, how were we fed? I remembered mornings when my brothers and I lined up at a small, plastic picnic table, its low bench in primary colors. Matt was almost six; Dave was four. I was seven, the oldest. The squad leader. Our father served breakfast: three paper bowls of oatmeal, three plastic spoons, three paper napkins. He let me pour the maple syrup.

I could smell Dad's aftershave through his crisp, white dress shirt; he taught science at a Catholic girls' high school. My mother, dressed for corporate computer programming in a shoulder-padded blazer, belted her trench coat against our oatmeal fingers. Before walking to the train station, she put on an extra coat of lipstick and kissed the backs of our hands. When we missed her at day care or school, we could look at her lipstick kisses. Our parents' marriage imploded the year I was seven, when she left our father in favor of the man who would become our stepfather.

On the convoy I shook my head and didn't throw the kids anything, though I had a bag of M&Ms and that sleeve of tasteless mashed potatoes I knew I would never eat. I told myself I had to set the example for the junior Marines. Still, I felt a wash of shame at refusing to feed those children and was grateful for the shaded goggles hiding my eyes.

Later a gunny told me the reason for the rules. He'd learned the hard way in Somalia. If you throw food, the kids climb the vehicles. When you have to move out fast, you inevitably run one over.

We pulled into Camp Scania, a supply contractors' base, just before sunset. This was supposed to be the easier of our two days on Iraq's roads, and IED rumors circulated about the next day's trip. Lieutenant Mosun, a young, blue-eyed military police officer who was half-Jordanian and all-gorgeous, gave an updated convoy brief. I didn't mind the excuse to look at him. He estimated it would take another long day of travel to get to our new base across the border. He reminded us of the dangerous cloverleaf near Fallujah. When the convoy before us had gotten hit, a few days earlier, they had waited several hours for Explosive Ordnance Disposal to clear them to move again. Or so the rumors went. We clung to scraps of plausible information, whether or not they'd prove accurate.

The military police company's first sergeant asked how I liked my first convoy so far. I told him I was frustrated with the begging kids and with the Marines for feeding them. I joked, "do not feed the animals," then instantly regretted it. *I shouldn't have said that*, I ruminated, shouldn't have denigrated those kids for playing on my sympathies, for exposing the gap between what I wanted to do and what I did. Should instead have encouraged the winning of hearts and minds, should have set the example. Still, I'd said it. I didn't make any move to take it back.

Lieutenant Mosun looked perturbed under his mustache, but the first sergeant laughed. He even repeated it during the safety brief: "Do not feed the animals!" The Marines roared.

In my bivy sack that night, on the ground next to our vehicle, I rolled this around in my head. Alienating Mosun was the last thing I wanted to do. "Maybe," I thought, "I should just throw food to the next kids we see." I rolled over, frustrated; my sleeping pad crunched gravel underneath. Throwing food wouldn't help—it'd be the exact opposite of what we'd just told our troops. So, like a good Marine, I summoned anger against my shame. "If it wasn't for those fuckin' hajjis," I thought, "we wouldn't have to be here." At the time, the word "hajji" didn't seem derogatory, to our minds—only *"fuckin'* hajji" did. Soon I would learn it was an honorific for one who had made the pilgrimage, or hajj, to Mecca. Years later I would realize how we'd perverted it into a slur. But that night, curled up on gravel, all I did was fall asleep.

In the predawn beehive of Velcroed vests and toothpaste-streaked spit, Marla found me. "I wish a terrorist had jumped out at us," she said.

"What?" I thought I'd heard her wrong.

"But a really dumb terrorist," she said. "And then we'd fire back and catch him. Then we'd get it over with."

Engine ignitions fired up as stars faded overhead. I guessed she had a point, breaking tension during the convoy's anxious monotony.

"And then we'd get our combat action ribbon," she said. It felt almost déclassé to mention ribbons immediately before stepping off on a convoy. A ribbon? Is that what we were there for? I was still fuzzy on the purpose of the war. Even now, when asked, I can't give a good solid reason.

When I was ordered to deploy, I didn't think about politics or oil or weapons of mass destruction or the tenuous—okay, nonexistent—link between Iraq and the attacks of September 11. I didn't think about saving people from a dictator; I'd been in fifth grade when Saddam had invaded Kuwait. Instead I focused only on what was in front of me and the people to my left and my right. I was a Marine; I was told to go somewhere, and so I went.

When faced with ambivalence, fear, and uncertainty, anger was a Marine's only admissible feeling, a standard emotional shortcut that made it okay to crack, "do not feed the animals." So I chose not to dwell on the justification—or lack thereof— for the Iraq War.

My responsibility was to the troops in my company—to not let them down. I just wanted to get back home, preferably without fucking up or making too much an ass of myself. Or dying. Not that, either. So, no, I didn't think about ribbons, and was suspicious of people who did.

Riding out, we passed a lump of fur on the road's shoulder— could have been a dead dog. Plastic litter and shredded sand-bags skipped in the wind. I held my breath at each pothole. *Can't outdrive an* IED. A few kids rode stumpy donkeys past more herds of camels and sheep, reminding me of a live Bible pageant. I had no idea people still lived like this. If I rewound the clock two thousand years, it would have looked the same.

North of Nasiriyah, no more kids begged. Old men turned their backs when they saw us coming. Buildings conjured an Arab South Bronx. Going through one village—a cluster of washed-out buildings, stacked milk crates by the curb—I glimpsed a booted shepherd grasping a wire-bound remote.

I aligned my rifle and clicked off the safety. When I squinted again, he just held an old man's cane.

We rolled on.

As we neared the cloverleaf on the outskirts of Fallujah, scraggly grass lay out past the concrete. This was the place, it was rumored, where the convoys before us had gotten ambushed. It looked the same as highway off-ramps back home, but I felt tense. People don't plant bombs on 1-95, under the signs for New Rochelle. Or by the Cambridge-Brighton split off the Mass Pike in Boston. I tried in vain to remember Basic School counter-ambush drills, trucks pulling off to alternate sides of the road, the admonition not to fire until we heard the machine guns.

I breathed deep as the overpass approached; my stomach clenched. We in our belching vehicles were the road's only travelers. I pictured our trucks toppled, columns of dirt exploding, like artillery simulators from the Basic School. I scanned the overpass, saw no one, and held my breath as we crossed under. We lumbered up the highway ramp. After, I would recall this curlicue of road as eerily quiet, though our Humvees must have roared, my temples must have pounded, and my breathing must have quickened. We sped away unmolested, exhaling through clouds of fine sand. We broke westward, away from Fallujah, toward our home for the next seven months.

We arrived at Camp Taqaddum—"TQ,"—thirsty and Chap-Sticked against wind and sun. Going through the gate, we cleared our weapons: magazine out, I aimed into a sand-filled barrel and pulled my trigger on an empty chamber. The angle was especially awkward because I was so short. Our Humvees and five-ton trucks rumbled up a long, gravel hill lined with broken chunks of concrete and human-height sand berms. Within a few minutes, we pulled into a clearing, and each driver inched up his vehicle's nose to the tail of the vehicle in front.

Our several-hundred-Marine convoy formed up in a semicircle around a no-nonsense female gunny for a "welcome brief," something like an orientation. The gunny stood on a stack of wooden pallets, brown hair in a curly mom-cut. I couldn't read the nametape on her uniform, its letters squished tight together. It began with B, long and hyphenated and Spanish. She launched into her in-brief, a staccato whirlwind of rules: when to carry flashlights (always), buddying up (as much as possible), and avoiding mortars (you can't). We could expect to get mortared, she said, maybe every few weeks to few days. Mortar blast craters measured fewer than ten feet across, but shrapnel could rip flesh thirty to fifty yards away. She detailed uniform rules for the chow hall: blouses (long-sleeved camouflage jackets) on, covers (hats) off. She told us to call her Gunny B.

Gunny B turned out to be one of my twenty-three female tentmates in the transient barracks, a gravel-bordered grid of kerosene-waterproofed tents. The locally sourced, double-layered tents had thick canvas shells and yellow cotton lining bordered in paisley. But my favorite discovery stood twenty yards away: trailers with porcelain toilets and reliable showers. A hygiene dream after several weeks of Kuwaiti Porta-Johns.

That first night, I walked the half-mile to the chow hall for a meal of steak, lobster, and crab legs. The meal seemed incongruous for a war zone—it *was* incongruous for a war zone, almost an affront to the barren plain "outside the wire," or off base— but contractors from Kellogg, Brown and Root had started this Saturday-night tradition, and we weren't about to stop them. Freezer cases lined the center aisle; I picked out strawberry ice cream. There were heated pools of melted butter and piles of exotic fruit. I selected an Asian pear. I would like to say that I thought sadly and meaningfully of the begging children from the day before. But I did not.

Instead I shoved my way down a long table and looked hard at my plate before tucking in. Buttered rice. Gristly maybe-beef and a tail of lobster I hadn't yet learned to deconstruct. Flimsy plastic plate, fork, spoon, knife. They all stood a good chance of

breaking if I attacked my meal too eagerly. The flatware was colored sandy beige, as if—set against an American flag-patterned
tablecloth in an airline-hangar-sized chow hall—it would better
camouflage us against the enemy. My mind still held a million
questions when faced with the next seven months, but the chow
hall's clamor that night approximated a block party. I mouthed
a tiny wooden paddle of ice cream, cautiously hopeful.

THREE

Groundhog Day

Camp Taqaddum, Iraq

The next morning, I trotted to Communications Company's compound—the comm site—a few hundred yards past the chow hall. On the way lay Tent City, acres of concrete filled by a grid of twelve-person tents. We'd move there from the transient barracks as soon as the army rotated off our base.

If Tent City were a football field, the chow hall would be on one sideline, the airfield on the other. One end zone held battalion headquarters, the chapel, a gym tent, and a few stores. Our PX, the Post Exchange, sold off-brand greeting cards, candy, and a half-dozen flavors of Gatorade. They sold DVDs, too, but no porn—for that you had to subvert our networks or bring your own on flash drives, or maybe ask the right guy fifty yards away in a row of locally staffed shops. There, Iraqis sold souvenir trinkets, bootleg DVDs, and fresh-cooked shawarmas and flatbreads. A few plastic tables provided a makeshift tea garden. Behind the market, a road arced around the huge flight line and runway toward "lakeside" TQ, the side of base that housed a battalion of maintenance Marines, engineers, and our ammunition supply point. The regimental headquarters and the comm site stood at the other end of the plateau—that is, the other end zone of TQ's football field.

Our mission at Comm Company was to expand radio, telephone, and data connectivity to all parts of twenty-seven-square mile TQ. Chief Warrant Officer Clive, whom I'd met briefly in California, had flown in a few weeks early with a skeleton crew. At the comm site, activity centered on Systems Control headquarters, or SYSCON: an unassuming concrete hut rumored to be a former torture chamber, where inscrutable Arabic graffiti had been scorched into the ceiling. Next to SYSCON, Marines had built scaffolding out of plywood and two-by-fours to climb up to various "vans"—olive green metal containers with heavy doors, mounted on massive truck platforms. Each van held equipment for data and telephone routing and switching, while dozens of reels of fiber optic cable stood stacked in front of them. Wire Platoon would be responsible for installing and maintaining it all. Marines streamed to and from twenty-foot embark containers, carrying telephones, wires, computers, encryption gear, and one printer that gave up the ghost as soon as someone plugged it in.

That first day, Captain Davis surprised me with my assignment for the next seven months: leading two platoons, both Wire and Maintenance, about thirty Marines in all. He introduced me to my staff noncommissioned officers, who'd come with Clive a few weeks prior to supervise the network infrastructure's initial setup. I shook hands with Staff Sergeant Garcia, my quiet, sinewy wire chief, and Gunny Lars, a compact former wrestler and my meticulous maintenance chief. Both were older than me; Gunny Lars was a seemingly ancient thirty-five. The staff NCOs had a solid decade more experience than I did and usually at least a bit of college. But after four years at MIT, a year and a half of basic officer and communications training, and going on seven weeks in the fleet, I was their boss, at least on the org chart.

As the junior-most officer, I also stood the SYSCON night watch, which started at 0200. Nervous about oversleeping and eager to avoid making a bad impression or getting my ass chewed by Captain Davis, I'd packed the loudest possible travel alarm clock, a free gift from my bank. The first night of SYSCON watch, it jolted me awake at 2300 with a nasal synth-pop rendition of the "William Tell Overture." By the second measure, I flailed and poked furiously at its thin vinyl buttons. By 2301 the alarm was off, and my chest exploded with adrenaline. Mortars could have awakened me more gently. The slender gunny whose cot sat a foot from mine must have been blessed with infinite patience. By the end of the first week, I could categorize each of my two dozen tentmates' watch-alarm beeps and keep them in spatial and chronological order. None was as intrusive as the goddamn "William Tell Overture." It replayed in my head every time I shook out a can of Gold Bond and thrust ragged toenails into wool socks.

Like many lieutenants, I straddled the line between gung-ho and idiocy when it came to exercise. Before midnight, I ran on the rough gravel roads, carrying a flashlight so trucks could spot me. Even with its bouncing beam, I could hardly see five feet ahead, and I tripped over concrete chunks, bruising my knees through OCS-issued sweats. I got up and kept running. Headlights higher than my head screamed toward me, and I scrambled off-road to avoid them. Trucks roared past, carrying water or sewage to or away from this place; I couldn't tell. I turned around and jogged back for a freezing shower.

Hurrying to the chow hall, I almost missed midrats, the meal for night-shifters. A fat, surly British cook, his scraggly hair thinner than his threadbare T-shirt, allowed me cold Weetabix and milk just before closing. Afterward, in the dark, I tried to stalk across the base to the SYSCON, shoulders up, chest out, like a He-Man cartoon. I stood five feet one and weighed a hundred and twenty-two pounds. Not at all bulletproof.

The SYSCON hut was so small that if I stretched my arms up, I could touch the ceiling. Tall Marines clocked their foreheads on the doorjamb. My watch chief, Staff Sergeant Gorman, ducked when he entered. His buddies called him Smiley Sam, because he was always in a good mood, even when everyone else was cranky and bitching. Not yet thirty years old, he already had smile lines at his eyes. We spent the night in SYSCON monitoring the network, making reports, answering emails, and swatting flies. When the base woke up, Captain Davis walked in, coffee in hand, awaiting his brief. Luckily, most nights were calm in those first few weeks. Smiley Sam and I would finish our watch at 1000, morning after morning, until they all blurred.

Meanwhile, during the day, my Marines tested myriad equipment. Antennas stalked up like fragile pines. My "wire dogs" dug trenches and ran cables to the regiment's buildings thirty yards away. They clipped Ethernet cables taut to walls in stark contrast to the army's sloppy spiderwebs. As network test lights blinked green, I felt proud of my hardworking troops.

Our responsibilities rose to provide connectivity for more units around the base. The network architecture grew exponentially. We were all sleep-deprived, but I spent afternoons with the staff NCOs, barely keeping up with the acronyms they threw at me, learning how our signal systems fit together. Microwaves leapt across ether. Electrons conducted down thin wires. Photons rattled through fragile fiber optics. The Marines made a "Troubleshooting Procedures" game out of a dartboard nailed to a plywood sheet. On the plywood, they drew Sharpied circles labeled, "quickly make up a believable answer," "surf internet," "take extended chow break," and "prank call Systems Control." We all took turns hurling dull darts. "If you hit a bull's-eye," one section claimed, "you actually have to troubleshoot the system!"

My troops talked in great detail about "*last* year," the "*real* war." As a new lieutenant in a unit made of people who'd deployed together eight months before, I had the constant impression of joining a summer camp the year after everyone else. I wondered if I would ever do anything measurably cool, like hack together a brilliant fix for maintaining connectivity under fire. Probably not. But, like most green lieutenants, I wanted everyone to like me, and I didn't want to screw up.

Clive, who'd become the company's operations officer in a

shuffle of responsibilities, pulled me outside for a smoke break. It didn't matter that I didn't smoke. He cupped his hands around a Marlboro, lit it, and said, "I been hearing you're real smart."

I shrugged.

"I heard you're funny, like, a real crazy lady. Why don't you talk to me?"

I shrugged again, thinking, *Dude, I just met you a month ago.* But a month meant forever in military time. Clive tried to draw me out by offering details of his own. He hailed from a few hours' drive from where I'd grown up in New York. He'd deployed to Somalia while I was in middle school. Back home, he drove a massive black truck; he jokingly called my Toyota Matrix a "chickmobile." Clive wasn't evil; he was very proficient in technical matters, and generous when explaining them. He did, however, enjoy reminding young lieutenants how much longer he'd been in the fleet.

Over the next few weeks, stress mounted in Comm Company. Though our job felt unglamorous, it seemed the war ran on electrons. The NIPRnet (the unsecured internet bearing CNN and emails home) and the SIPRnet (the secure internet showcasing friendly grid coordinates, KIA reports, and intelligence briefings) provided the base's heartbeat. Angry field-grade officers at regimental headquarters wanted their email blazing at all hours, no matter the sandstorms. All ranks noticed when our overtaxed generators, clogged with sand and low on fuel, broke down. Marines couldn't phone, couldn't surf their precious internet, couldn't send messages back and forth in their endless reporting through the chain of command. When a web page wouldn't reload—even if, in the grand scheme of things, it was *just a web page*—the easiest thing for the colonels to do was take it out on us.

In the midst of this, Clive couldn't agree with my staff NCOs on the plan to lay the thirty kilometers of fiber optic cable necessary to tie in the whole base. He argued sternly, mustache twitching, while Staff Sergeant Garcia and our master sergeant, or "Top," cast sidelong glances at each other. Too inexperienced to be sure of the best course of action, I didn't offer an opinion during these arguments.

But since I was quick on the uptake, "smart," as Clive said, I soon scored a promotion of sorts—standing watch during the main part of the day: 1000 to 1800. It meant a vote of confidence from Captain Davis, but it also meant more pressure. Daytime was the busiest time, and the prize for winning the pie-eating contest was more pie.

I showed up at chow early one morning, 0530 or 0600, and found Captain Davis and Clive sitting across from each other at the chow hall, talking intensely. I sat down and smiled, "Morning, gentlemen," I said, "How's it going?"

He glowered at me. "Where were you this morning?"

I held my hard-boiled egg, poised to crack it. "Sir?"

"Huge generator outage, about 0300. Why weren't you there?"

Sand had clogged the generator, and my Marine had let it run out of fuel. Why wasn't I there, on the spot, when it went down?

"Sir, I was—I was racked out."

"Why did I have to find out from someone else, T?"

"I didn't know, sir." I had had no idea it had happened. I'd been on my cot, stone asleep.

"It's fixed now, but don't let it happen again," he huffed. He finished his forkful, stood, and left.

"You're lucky you weren't there at 0530 when he found out," Clive said, *sotto voce*, as he got up. Though their words were few, it felt like a tag-team reprimand. I smacked my egg on the table, peeled it, and choked down a few bites. Not hungry. I gathered my CamelBak and hustled to Maintenance Platoon's can, where the gunny had already doled out the requisite scoldings and scheduled a twenty-four-hour watch to prevent any of the Marines from letting a generator run out of fuel again.

Still, I could not stand the feeling of the captain's disapproval or Clive's head-shaking. A platoon's failures are its leader's failures, regardless of whether the leader actually knows about them, or who is actually at fault. If you are a Marine officer, your job is to ensure mistakes are not made, or if they are made, to be fully accountable. You can delegate responsibility, but never accountability. It all comes back on your shoulders. In the civilian world, you can go home after a day's work, pop open a beer, and relax. In Iraq, your boss can thrust his head through your tent flap at midnight if you're delinquent. You're always on the job.

To control as much as possible, I hewed to a strict routine: the same chow-hall breakfast, the same daily workout, showering in one specific stall, a lunchtime burger, visiting Wire Platoon, then the maintenance area, without fail. For my unwillingness to explore other options, Marla nicknamed me Rain Man.

In a move that would eventually backfire, I navigated our company's power dynamics through constant appeasement. When tactical disagreements arose, I let my head be turned by each debater. Clive wanted the cable laid one way? Okay, sure, he was a chief warrant officer with eighteen years' experience. Garcia thought it should be another way? Well, he was in the trenches, he knew best . . . until Clive came down again, asked why the Marines weren't doing it his way. I could not win, and yet I felt too unqualified—and conflict-averse—to make the call on my own. I was, after all, a twenty-three-year-old second lieutenant, with six months of classroom training but virtually no field experience. I did not yet know that all second lieutenants were unsure of themselves, that everyone navigated steep learning curves differently—and just how close to burnout my compulsive people-pleasing would bring me.

In the end, while Clive was distracted by other tasks, I let my Marines run their own show, giving Gunny Lars, Staff Sergeant Garcia, and Smiley Sam orders only after they leaned in with knowing "suggestions." My scrambling didn't finish the job any faster—it only layered exhaustion on top of my guilt.

We were miles from combat, but its reminders came in fits and starts. We snapped photos of each other near the regimental headquarters, in front of a shot-out mural of Saddam Hussein. Someone had scrawled the word "BUMFIGHTS" across his forehead. Soon enough, we took multiple mortar rounds, one of which broke a corporal's arm. The enemy's aim was improving, but if you could observe the explosion's impact, it meant you weren't hit.

One evening a rocket attack occurred just past my bedtime. I stood sock-footed in the tent, pulling on trousers, flak jacket, and helmet. Gunny B pounced through the rows of cots, counting us. She looked alert but unrattled. After the last six rounds detonated in quick succession, she told us they were friendly, from counterbattery radar—the Marines who triangulated the insurgents' positions and fired back. She told me to get some sleep. Like hell I could.

That first month, I had trouble sleeping; I was too keenly aware of being a scrap of skin in thin T-shirt and shorts wormed into a soft sleeping bag. Fabric couldn't guard against every threat. Rape, bullets, shrapnel, knives: all seemed possibilities, and my body rioted at its vulnerability. Fear turned to rage. Nights, I tossed with dreams of being chased by a violent enemy. I shouted in my sleep, "I'll kill you!" then woke thrashing on my cot, breath ragged, heart pounding. I squirmed facedown, eyes squeezed shut, hoping no one would notice. No one ever did.

Grim hyperalertness became my default mode; upon getting my emails, my old lab partner from college said I sounded "mad at the world." One afternoon between watch and sleep, I ducked into an empty chapel tent and sat down on a pile of sandbags. Those were the first few moments I had alone—truly alone, where no one knew to find me—in the month since we'd left California. I felt profoundly sorry for myself, but couldn't pinpoint why.

I sat on those sandbags bewildered as to how I'd wound up in Iraq. At eighteen years old, raising a hand for my midshipman oath with chopped-off hair and a stained button-down, I'd had plans to pay for college and stay in shape. Learning to blow things up had seemed fun. Senior year, the September

11 attacks had given us more of a tutorial in explosions than I'd ever imagined. Before then, I hadn't thought through what would happen if we landed in this wartime parallel universe. I wanted, more than ever—more than at any summer camp, college dorm, or training barracks—to be back under my blankets, in a quiet room, in America.

Tears came quickly. I pressed my knuckles to my eyes and sobbed into balled fists. I breathed through my mouth, feeling alternately sorry for myself and ashamed. Warriors shouldn't feel this way, I thought. I consciously slowed my breathing, let my eyes adjust to the dimness. At least now there were neither mortars nor angry comrades stalking by. I had these few minutes of quiet solitude. Sunbeams streaked in where the tent flap met the rest of the canvas. I let myself cry until snot dripped on the sand-grazed deck.

I inhaled a few ragged breaths and horked the contents of my dribbling snout into napkins stolen from the chow hall. I rubbed my wrist over wet eyes, adjusted my glasses, stood up. Figured I'd sniveled enough to survive the next couple of days. Pulling open the tent flap, I blinked back afternoon sun. Maybe if I threw myself at my tasks with rabid intensity, no one could disapprove of me, and I could outrun pain. As I walked towards the chow hall, I rallied my old friend anger to combat my shame and mask my weakness. It was better to be pissed off than weak, even if it meant harboring indiscriminate rage at the Iraqis, at senior officers, at myself. I stomped my boots, reciting the antiwar e.e. cummings poem "i sing of olaf glad and big" in a fit of secret rebellion. "I will not kiss your fucking flag," I thought. Except I had no choice. The flag already flew overhead.

FOUR

Hometown Throwdown

Suburban New York

I had long known the virtue of hiding tears. Saturday mornings when I was seven, Dad would pick up Matt, Dave, and me while Mom waved us good-bye from behind a brittle smile. When we kids weren't in our apartment, she spent weekends with the man for whom she'd divorced Dad, the days penned "NO KIDS" on the kitchen calendar.

On those Saturdays, Dad took us to the deli, smokes and food his first order of business. He was loyal to the cigarette brand True. "True blues," he'd say across the counter, an unspoken coda etched into his frown: *not like your mother*. Then he'd get us all egg-and-cheese sandwiches. If, in our rambunctiousness, one of us knocked over a glass of water, he'd angrily wipe the spill, muttering, "pigs," through gritted teeth. After, when he asked where we wanted to go, Matt and Dave would invariably shout, "toy store!" and off we'd drive. The boys were thrilled; I was embarrassed. "Go on, pick something out," Dad would say as I shuffled down the aisle, as if Legos or a craft set would shrink the lump in my throat, erase the memory of his set jaw and fist clenched around napkins. When Matt kicked and whined in the car's backseat outside our local five-and-dime, Dad shook him by the shoulders.

On the ride to his apartment, Dad lectured, "your father

provides for you," always in the third person. He harangued us about how Mom was sleeping with another man, how illegal—*against the law! Church law!*—it was that this man slept at our apartment. Which laws Mom had broken, I never understood.

Dad's apartment sported three sleeping bags on the floor, a backyard with a turtle-shaped sandbox, and a lady downstairs who pounded on the ceiling whenever we made noise, which was always. Most weekends there, I couldn't stop crying; I wanted my mom. Dad let me call her, but she said I had to stay. "Wash your pretty little face," she said. "Go play with your brothers." I sat mute in front of the TV, Dad's all-purpose anesthetic. Sunday evenings, he'd return us, like foster puppies.

On the rare occasions I could stanch my torrential emotions, I concentrated on shepherding my brothers, on procuring us snacks, on flipping morning pancakes like a tiny adult-in-training. It took a couple of years before I learned to shut down any sensitivity, revealing only a mask of silent compliance. This was the only way, anymore, to be loved.

In the years before he married my stepmother, my father had several girlfriends. One was Cheryl, blond and shimmering in the front seat while Dad drove his new silver sedan to the annual car show at the Javits Center. Matt, Dave, and I were strapped in the back. We flipped the ashtray covers in the rear door handles. For once, we didn't whip each other with the buckle ends of our seat belts. Perhaps we hadn't even yet stained the upholstery with juice and gum. Instead we gawked at the buildings along the West Side Highway and cringed at the men wielding squeegees on 42nd Street. At the exhibition, Matt and Dave ran between sports cars as Cheryl tottered in heels. Though we had a good time that day, riding sugar highs and staring at Detroit's latest concepts, we wouldn't see Cheryl again.

The following Saturday, Dad's leather jacket creaked as he turned around from the wheel to face us; we were about to pick up another of his dates, Elaine. When I think of my dad in the late eighties and early nineties, he's with a series of women, always wearing that jacket. "Now, children," he said, "Elaine doesn't need to know about Cheryl."

A year or so later, he took us to a girlfriend's family's upstate pizza parlor. Before the drive, Dad bought us each toys. I colored a basketball jersey on my yellow vinyl dinosaur before wolfing a slice of Sicilian. That night we stayed in a hotel. Matt and Dave had one bed; Dad had the other. I recall lying down on the thin brown carpet. I can't remember if the woman stayed.

These women were uniformly nice to us and seemed to think we were cute even when we misbehaved. Maybe they were just humoring Dad. I wonder now why he didn't confine his dates to weeknights or weekends when we weren't with him. Maybe he was auditioning new wives, fake mothers. Trying to replace, as quickly as possible, the loss of his family.

• • •

Dad's toy-store bribes were not without use. One Saturday morning shortly after I turned eight, he bought me my first baseball glove. He threw ball after ball, teaching me, Matt, and Dave to throw, catch, field, and bat in the leaf-strewn yard behind his apartment. He pitched overhand, never underhand, and though initially I found the speeding rubber ball intimidating, I soon learned to angle my mitt and bat correctly. He never got angry when we played baseball, just pitched and caught and shagged our wobbly pop flies.

My new glove came in handy at my Catholic school's recess. While the few other girls played tag, I ran around with a pack of boys, the lone plaid jumper in a sea of gray flannel pants and white shirts. With my pageboy haircut and Peter Pan collar, slight overbite, and knee-high red socks, I was the third-grade tomboy. When our mob split in two across a parking lot, a single tennis ball sufficed for a game of catch. The most effeminate boy stood to one side, keeping score: a point for each uncaught throw. I liked the game's rhythm, the green ball arcing against white clouds, the triumph of its clean *pock* in my mitt.

Amid the boys, I felt plainspoken ease—their acceptance lay in simply catching the ball and throwing it hard. They favored shoving over storytelling, with none of the secret-keeping and mysterious teasing that characterized my girl classmates' play. When my brothers and I moved to public school the following year (our mother's cash had run low, and our school's nuns harped on her about the divorce), I toted my trusty mitt to the playground, wearing jeans—ripped and patched and ripped again—and a pink skateboarding sweatshirt. An auburn-haired fellow tomboy, Danielle, soon became my best friend; she resembled the Peanuts character Peppermint Patty. Our agility and speed won us friends among the boys and cheerful approval from our male teacher.

By then our mother was engaged to marry the man who would become our stepfather. For about two years now, when Mom took Matt, Dave, and me into local restaurants, she would say hello to the same man eating alone—plain pasta with olive oil, no garlic. His name was Bruce; he was five feet one and bald, with a chinstrap beard. He wore corduroy pants, and sometimes suits. Mom knew him, was excited to see him, and he to see her. He'd ask us kids for high-fives by way of hello and would tell a corny joke or two as Mom settled into his booth. We'd have a "kids' booth" behind them. We didn't mind; we liked having the space to ourselves. It took me decades to realize they could have arranged this ahead of time, that it might not have been just coincidence that we kept showing up to the same places.

By the time I hit middle school, Bruce and Mom had been married a year. Faced with three kids at home and a son of his own he rarely saw, he fired fewer mortars than Al-Qaeda would, but his level of anger was about the same. He required us to ask permission to go outside, to turn on the TV or computer, or to get a snack from the refrigerator. We had to be fully dressed before leaving our rooms in the morning; if, say, Dave tied his shoelaces in the living room, or I came out still pulling on a sweater over my T-shirt, Bruce yelled at us to get back in our rooms for "not being dressed." He patrolled the apartment, still wet from the shower, wearing only a towel. Grinding us down with circular reasoning, he repeated, "I'm not punishing you; you're punishing yourself," after some infraction of the Byzantine rules. We weren't stupid. We understood consequences. But we also understood that control was all he wanted.

By then I navigated power dynamics at school, too. One popular girl in my sixth-grade cafeteria, a paragon of early '90s fashion, wore acid-washed jeans and crimped her hair. I recall hot-pink rubber bands linking her braces as she snickered, "you look like a boy" in response to my New York Giants sweatshirt and ponytail. Though I wore backwards baseball caps and baggy jeans, I would eventually get my ears pierced specifically so people could tell I was a girl.

Dad had given me a pink-and-black spiral Nerf, and at recess Danielle and I played tackle football with a pack of boys. But this became about more than just the game. As my male classmates sprouted muscles, I smelled Right Guard and Old Spice in the huddle. One boy, sideburned and muscular in a white T-shirt, diagrammed plays on his palm with a finger, his wavy bangs gelled up and away from his face. I didn't pay any attention to the strategy, just him and the other boys around me. Despite my pint-sized stature, I became the most aggressive defensive tackle on the playground.

I never flirted, not even during failed tackles, when bigger boys sometimes carried me down the field, my small arms near-choking them, my leg clinched around their waists. They treated my stubborn clinging as part of the football game—nothing more. And it was easier for me to ignore them, too, rather than risk the vulnerability of flirting. I avoided eye contact and wore baggy shirts with Yankees logos and nondescript J.C. Penney jeans. Even if I found certain boys attractive, I almost never mentioned that fact out loud, even in loose-leaf notes folded in triangles and passed to Danielle and other girlfriends between classes, or gel-penned and mailed over summer break.

Sometime during my middle-school years, my brothers, earnest Cub Scouts, became obsessed with camping. On a hometown street we'd never before explored, their little jaws dropped at the camouflage gear in the Marine recruiting station's window. They pestered Mom until we all entered. The recruiter, a tall African American Marine in blood striped pants and a khaki shirt, said, "We have scholarships; come back when you're seventeen," and gave us posters I soon aligned on my bedroom wall. I liked the uniforms. I liked the weapons. I loved the intimation of power—power of which Matt, Dave, and I possessed little at home.

When I was fourteen, Bruce tried to force Matt, then twelve, into pajamas for a punishingly early bedtime on a Friday night. Likely Matt had uttered some bit of rudeness. Mom, equally angry as Bruce, followed them into the boys' room. I heard her weight brace the door closed from the inside. I retreated into my room next door; I was waiting for Danielle to pick me up. Her grandfather had promised to take us ice-skating. Dave sat in the living room; he might have been watching TV.

I lay in bed on the same Strawberry Shortcake sheets I'd had since kindergarten and heard Matt's refusal to change into pajamas. I put on my headphones to drown out Bruce's staccato commands: Beethoven's Ninth Symphony, the only cassette tape I owned. Through the music I heard a clank, a shout. A shaft of hall light shone through my cracked-open door, my only illumination. Should I get up and see what they were doing to my brother? I shifted; the white metal daybed creaked under my weight. I turned up my Walkman. I can't remember whether Dave turned up the TV.

Next door I heard the bang of something being knocked over. Matt shouted "No!" and Bruce yelled something louder. If I tried to burst in, Mom would push me back, I was sure of it— just as Matt and Dave had closed that same door on me during our petty fights. To compound it, then she and Bruce would be mad at me—and we all knew the kind of shit that happened when Bruce got mad at you.

Now Bruce was trying to strip Matt's clothes. Matt fought back, fairly strapping for twelve years old, but still at least an inch shorter and twenty pounds lighter than Bruce. I heard another clank and shout, the sound of the metal bunk bed sliding. Matt must have grabbed it for leverage.

I turned up Beethoven's violins and timpani, but I could still hear Matt say, "Mom!"

"That's enough, Bruce," my mom said. "That's enough," she said again. And again. Each time louder. But she wouldn't get in between them. And Bruce would not stop.

Eventually they came out of the room. I turned off the music. I heard Matt sobbing.

When Danielle knocked at the front door at the appointed time, I grabbed my jean jacket and bolted. "Fucking zoo," I muttered outside, taking lungfuls of icy air. But I told her nothing more of what had just happened. I didn't want to complicate the night, didn't want to be an object of concern or gossip—and didn't want to tell the story of how I'd listened to my brother get beaten, and hadn't done anything.

Today I know that expecting a lightweight, fourteen-year-old girl to defend her brother against a grown man was, at best, unrealistic. But when I saw the nosebleed stains on Matt's mattress the morning after the incident, I felt even worse for letting him thrash alone.

I especially didn't want to look weak in front of Danielle or any other classmates. The year before, they had conspired to publicize a crush of mine—and my subsequent rejection—to half the eighth grade. I didn't have the social savvy to counter this public-shaming rite of passage, the relational aggression with which girls' claws sharpen into women's. I learned only this: girls weaponized words. Girls betrayed. Girls exploited emotional vulnerability to wage psychological warfare. I understood physical warfare better—especially after what had happened at home. So I made myself more like a boy, adopting a perma-scowl and tackling even harder in subsequent playground football matches.

Better to talk with boys there, even if only in shouts of *onegatortwogatorthreegatorfourgator* before shoving them to the dirt. Running and throwing and huddling, I could at least be close to them—even if the price was denying everything I felt. Further shame at the hands of my classmates was something I couldn't afford. I'd gotten enough of powerlessness at home.

The classroom, my sanctuary, rewarded my knack for jumping through overachiever hoops. Marching band, varsity softball, Advanced Placement courses, nationals on the academic team all four years of high school. Accomplishments brought me teachers' approval and attention. If I squinted, it felt like love.

The band room enveloped me, too. When my high school band director, Ms. Hopper, gave me her full attention to rehearse difficult measures or make a joke, I felt starstruck. She was a practical woman, single-handedly completing carpentry projects and building elaborate Halloween decorations. One year she enlisted Matt, me, and our friends to help her deck out her house. I lay under a tree, wearing a headset borrowed from the school stage crew, to relay to her the costumes of trick-or-treaters coming down the sidewalk. She sat in a darkened window with a microphone and spoke to the kids in ghostly voices. She also masterminded school pranks, once hosting a dozen kids in a weekend-long papier-mâché session to secretly build a twenty-foot model of a human colon. In rehearsal, when her baton sliced downward and sideways, home fell away, and I felt safe.

At a cast party after a high school musical performance, several years past my middle-school ostracism, I tried on a formfitting, scoop-necked brown shirt—likely something from Abercrombie or J. Crew or the Gap, nothing scandalous. My friends cheered. The hottest guy in the cast, a teenage Italian Adonis who outdanced everyone, called me beautiful. Their attention unnerved me, and I couldn't exchange the shirt fast enough for the flannel in which I'd arrived. I was used to seeming smart or strong; though girls and guys had all said kind things, feminine allure didn't feel like power.

Senior year, college loomed, and my parents had long since burned through their savings divorcing each other. I'd saved several thousand dollars as a babysitter and camp counselor, but it wasn't nearly enough. I remembered the recruiter's enticement. Four of the schools to which I applied offered ROTC scholarships: full tuition, free books, and a guaranteed job after graduation. The Marine Corps looked badass, and I wanted to be a badass. Besides, it was 1997. It wasn't like we were at war.

Dad enthusiastically supported my ROTC application. In addition to the monetary lure, he'd always revered pomp and parades, order and routine. He never missed an opportunity to photograph my brothers and me in uniform, whether for Scouts, sports, or marching band. He himself had never served; his hearing aids had made him ineligible for Vietnam. Instead, he'd joined the seminary, then left it at twenty-six, trading cassock for a teacher's blazer and tie.

But because my mother had custody of me, and I was only sixteen, she had to sign my application form. The first time I approached her, sitting on our stained living-room sofa, she balked. "You're just doing this for the money," she said, in her brook-no-bullshit voice. I figured I had about a minute before I truly pissed her off.

"It's not just the money," I said. "I really want to do this." Meaning escape.

Her face changed then. It looked about to crumple, and I saw I'd misjudged her reaction. "I'm afraid they'll whisk you off to some boot camp, and I'll never see you again," she said, her voice breaking. I was surprised that she cared. My half brother Zach was by then a year old, and Matt and Dave were rowdy teenagers. There were plenty of days when, distracted by the baby and Bruce, it felt like she didn't want the rest of us. Ultimately, though, she couldn't argue with the money ROTC would provide.

A week before the program began, I got a short haircut. I cried afterward, running a hand over the blank nape of my neck and feeling unlike myself. I didn't know how much else I'd lose, or what I'd gain. I just wanted to prove my worth, pay for college— and get the hell away from my stepfather. If the Corps would just fund my schooling to help me escape, I'd pledge them years of my life. Easy trade.

In a high-school graduation card, Matt wrote, "Stay another year? Please?"

I hugged my brothers good-bye and left for MIT.

Training

Cambridge, Massachusetts

Freshman year, I pulled my first all-nighter to write a paper in the hours before my first field training exercise. No explanation preceded the seven-mile conditioning hike on that hot fall morning. Carrying an ill-fitting pack while wearing new boots and a stiff camouflage uniform, I thought, "Where are we going, what are we doing, and why does this hurt so much?" I fell behind, ran to catch up, got nickel-sized blisters, and sweated buckets. I couldn't keep up for long; a few miles in, one of the staff quietly collected me and put me in a van.

Most of the twenty other Marine midshipmen were men. The few other women were juniors and seniors—and a foot taller than me. One, a sinewy Harvard rower, would later try out for the Olympics, while another muscular brunette had just graduated from Officer Candidates School. She was high up in the Boston Naval ROTC Consortium's chain of command and could hike endlessly, it seemed, without breaking a sweat. I felt too intimidated to ask for advice.

By November I hadn't yet finished a hike and was failing physics, my intended major. At Dad's for Thanksgiving weekend, he thought it would be funny to wake me at 0700 by blasting reveille on his stereo. He didn't seem to understand why I'd want to sleep in. But I had a bigger surprise for him. I'd started

dating my first boyfriend, Nathan, another freshman in ROTC.
A former cross-country runner, he was a quiet triple-major in
economics, international relations, and political science. To my
surprise, he'd liked me for weeks before asking me to practice
for the swim qualification with him. When we discovered the
pool was closed, we walked miles from Cambridge to Boston's
South End, ate midnight pizza, and talked until dawn.

Nathan and I kept our relationship quiet around the unit.
Plenty of midshipmen dated each other, but we had a tight-knit
class, and I felt that I had to keep up a professional mask. We
even emailed each other in navy memo format. Along with our
other classmates, Nathan helped me train in rope climbing, hik-
ing, and running. One freezing winter Saturday, he joined me
for a practice hike with a pack along the Charles River. As we
crossed the last bridge, we could hear ice tinkling on the water
below. I likely would have quit the five-mile loop without him.

But no matter how hard I tried that winter, I still couldn't
climb a rope. There came a point in every workout when it wasn't
a matter of if I would quit climbing; it was a matter of when.
Officer Candidates School would require me to have mastered
rope climbing within the next two years, and enough midshipmen struggled with this that needing remediation wasn't typically shameful. But at seven in the morning in that gym full of
military men, little felt worse than being the one woman who
couldn't climb the braided hemp.

By winter I grew desperate enough to ask a few classmates
for help. One, who would later become a navy helicopter pilot,
taught me a technique to grip the rope between my boots. She
mentioned I should squeeze the rope between my knees, too—
anything to stay on it. It worked.

The last winter workout of the season, in front of all the
Marine midshipmen, I climbed the rope to the spot at which
I usually quit. I looked straight ahead, willing my muscles—
and my mind—not to fail. I gripped the rope hard, squeezed

my knees, raised up my legs and kept climbing. I smacked the dusty pipe at the top and let out my loudest yell.

The following summer's training spanned two weeks in the Mojave Desert to observe a combined arms exercise, which evaluated an infantry battalion's combat capabilities. I joined about two dozen other midshipmen, seven of whom were also women.

At Twentynine Palms we watched a company close with its target and call in mortars on bombed-out vehicles. We hung out for an afternoon with a squad of snipers. All combat arms specialties—from firing rockets to driving armored vehicles— were open only to men. But our instructor, a former Force Recon captain, made no mention of gender when assigning tasks; we all hiked the same terrain and carried the same weight, and everyone looked identical in helmets and load-bearing vests.

We traded jokes and stories during days full of hurry-up-and-wait. Schooled since childhood in the ways of boys, I told my favorite in a Scottish accent. The punchline involved a sex act and a goat. My male comrades found this hilarious. When we got ice cream bars in the evening heat, I made a show of calculating how fast they could melt, willingly cultivating a nerdy, androgynous image. One male colleague called me "lepton," a joke cribbed from the child-prodigy movie *Little Man Tate*. Others just called me "MIT."

At night in the field, sleeping locations were set not by gender, but by four-person fireteam. On sandy gravel, we rolled out our sleeping bags, taking turns standing watch. Male midshipmen slept on either side of me. It was no big deal. I heard stories from the other women about their classmates who'd slept around the previous summer. But that wasn't me, nor was it the case for most female midshipmen I knew. Even though Nathan and I would break up several months later, ROTC did not provide its participants with an unlimited dating pool.

Soon I met a fellow hockey player on a D-league intramural team. He was our grad-student ringer, a power forward studying quantum computation. With a backwards baseball cap, perpetual wisecracks, and a close-cropped goatee, he presented a cross between Adam Sandler and David Duchovny. When he invited me to his apartment, I wore the brown undershirt to my camouflage uniform, and it wasn't until he said he liked it that I noticed it showed, from certain angles, hints of my curves. After a cursory glance at the movie *The Cutting Edge*—I was old enough to drink, but even now can't recall whether we shared a beer—we made out, then moved to his bed. In the coming weeks, I phoned him over and over, not realizing that even early versions of cell phones had a missed call log. My puppy-ish antics halted the next time I saw him, when in the midst of some fumbled groping, he prematurely ended the evening with the words *you're so awkward.*

Mortified, I left his studio in Copley Square and walked across the Charles River, back to campus, alone and convinced I always would be.

Solitude wasn't always a disadvantage; I parlayed my heart-break into working harder. Senior year, my short legs could churn through a fifteen-mile conditioning hike, and I could climb a rope while wearing a helmet and flak jacket. The summer prior, at Officer Candidates School, our most fearsome sergeant instructor had lined up all sixty of us female candidates at attention. Our first overnight liberty was to start the following morning. If we behaved, we got thirty-six hours off. Staff Sergeant Dunford, a compact African American woman, paced in front of us, her polished boots shining against our freshly mopped floor. Her speech was as sharp as the creases in her immaculate uniform.

"If you a woman in the Marine Corps," she snarled, "you either a bitch, a dyke, or a ho."

My eyes widened. I'd tuned out many ass-chewings, but I was definitely paying attention now.

"If you always gotta be with the males, an' you *smiling* at them, and every time you talk to them you gotta touch they *arm*"— she raised an index finger—"then you a ho."

"But if you do yo' *job*, and you treat them like they yo' *brother*, but you don't pay no attention to them 'cause *you* got a man some-whey *else*?" She spun around.

"*Then* you a bitch."

"That last one," she said, "I don't think I need to explain."

But could we really be reduced to just three categories? There was so much variety in our platoon of women. One prior enlisted candidate was a former drill instructor herself. Many were college kids too young to legally drink: varsity athletes, military brats, and lost souls outrunning childhood trauma. True, we had two boob job recipients: one enlargement, one reduction. And half of us had tattoos, but only one had tattooed-on eyeliner. All of us sported gruesome bruises. A few were mothers. Fewer were atheists. Two did turn out to be gay. Evangelical Christians prayed to recover from injuries and colds. Lapsed Catholics feigned devotion to sit for half an hour at Mass. Some used vocal fry to project an aura of command. Others had naturally deep voices, like the one at whom an instructor yelled, "Candidate, you need to stop smoking cigars and drinking cheap whiskey!"

Still, that sweaty summer, I couldn't envision our platoon commander, Captain Jansen, as a bitch, dyke, or ho. During the school year, she was the Marine Officer Instructor at a Midwest university. She'd been one of the first female helicopter pilots in the Marine Corps; her call sign echoed a popular TV show's warrior princess. At six feet tall, hair tucked in a neat French braid, she could handily complete the obstacle course without using any of the ramps typically afforded to females. She served a different purpose from the sergeant instructors who drove us, dervish-like, with calculated sadism. Even-tempered and dry-humored, Captain Jansen was firm but encouraging.

She never mentioned the "bitch-dyke-ho" speech—she hadn't been there that night—but she alluded to similar themes in a brief formation during our final week. She explained how the active-duty Marine Corps environment was much different from our university ROTC units. "You'll meet guys you like," she said. "You might even meet someone you want to date. But don't date anyone in your company. And for God's sake, not in your platoon!"

Her message was clear: if we felt any spark of attraction, we'd better keep it far away from our daily routine.

SIX

Night Watch

Camp Taqaddum, Iraq, Deployment Day plus Six Weeks

Marla had heard the same speeches at OCS. She stood the SYSCON watch right before mine and stuck around to chat afterward with Sam and me and whoever else was awake. She spoke of her own childhood, a global hopscotch with her Brazilian-born mother, three sisters, and financier father: middle school on one continent, early high school on another, waxing and waning Catholicism. One last move to the States, an international college career. She could speak three languages and studied Arabic on the side. Growing up in New York, I'd learned only some high-school Italian. No use for it in Iraq.

I discussed little, if any, of my childhood background with Marla and Sam during those late nights—doing so would have made me feel exposed. Instead I stuck to network status reports and helped Sam assemble an mp3 playlist. Our favorite was Outkast's "Hey Ya"; for the length of the song, we could pretend to be ordinary twentysomethings. A friend of mine had emailed a video of cartoon characters dancing to it, which inspired Marla to anoint the 0400 hour "SYSCON Dance Party." Sam thrust his fists in a circle for a few beats, attempting the Cabbage Patch. I sat stiffly, my smile pasted on, and didn't even try to move to the music. I knew the social liability of my lack of rhythm, and I never again, in any context, wanted to hear the words *you're so awkward.*

Marla danced in her T-shirt and camo pants, desert boots sure-footed on concrete, thermal sweatshirt folded into a turban. She bopped her head and may even have shimmied her shoulders, but never thrust her hips. She laughed and mouthed the lyrics, breaking the monotony of spreadsheets and reports and uncooperative signal equipment. She'd been awake since the previous morning; everyone got a little loopy this late. Sam and I munched care-package candy and MRE bread. Usually it was just we three, though sometimes a corporal would wander in to make a report from the data tent. He'd lower his gaze when he saw Marla dancing. He'd sit in a metal folding chair for a few minutes, try to get Sam's attention, and wait to speak as Marla's lithe frame moved. He would try, and fail, not to stare at her. The corporal returned to the watch hut a few nights in a row after that, staying longer each time, never dancing himself.

On those nights after SYSCON Dance Party, when it was just she, Sam, and I, Marla talked about her fiancé. She wore an emerald ring from a stateside lieutenant who stitched himself homemade ghillie suits—camo-net clothing of yarn and leaves—but would not propose properly. It had been several weeks since she'd gotten an email from him, but at least his last card had been a love letter.

On the surface, I stayed mission-focused, content to let Marla spill her romantic troubles. Inside, I stewed. One night, while our playlist bleated "Every Rose Has Its Thorn," I decided it was a good idea to email the hockey player with whom I'd fooled around in college. Back then, I'd liked him far more than he'd liked me, but now he wrote me back within a day. This was a perk of deployment; people worried about you. But I didn't get more than a line or two from him. Instead, I got mail from Ben, a guy I'd dated in Quantico before I left for California. We were still on friendly terms, but his cards held no lovesick confessions, just the antics of Peanut, his hamster. Still, they were something from home—and the closest I got to romance. I tried to feel more affection for him, but my heart wasn't in the card I sent back.

I dashed off a perky note, wrote "free" in the envelope's corner in lieu of a stamp, and tossed it into the basket to be mailed. I told Sam and Marla nothing of these quasi-romances. In the stoic-Marine mode I'd adopted, I figured admitting attraction would just make me look weak.

But when Marla spoke, men noticed, despite her engagement ring. How could they ignore her, with her red braid, her graceful gait, her willingness to dance? At chow, she discussed international politics and her fiancé's letters with equal enthusiasm. In return, the men stared at her thin olive T-shirt from across the table. A lieutenant colonel stopped her near regimental headquarters in order to compliment her appearance. Another officer from the air wing sauntered by daily to "ask about the crypto," hoping Marla would flirt with him. Forget the nuances of communication in civilian life; on a base in Iraq, perception was reality. Marla's emotional openness made her appear available. And when the men found they could not claim her, their attention curdled into contempt.

It continued when she briefed her platoon. In the weekly briefs called "platoon commander's time," we lieutenants established our presence, passed word on base policies, or taught useful classes. She introduced herself by saying that she didn't want to be a communications officer, that she disliked the field. She didn't mean to knock the entire occupational specialty, one in which her Marines excelled. She meant instead to highlight her desire to be a leader rather than a comm nerd, that she was there for the Marines themselves rather than the electronics. But her technical-expert senior enlisted took her words to mean that she didn't care at all. They'd say her name with a barely perceptible eye roll. When she announced during her next "platoon commander's time" that she was offering a poetry class in the evenings, they might even have suppressed snickers from the back row.

Seeing this, I took pains to cultivate a warrior image. It helped that I did love comm, and eagerly soaked up tidbits about routers and switches; this focus on technical competence kept most conversations impersonal. To show my Marines I was one of them, I trooped around our compound, poking my head into maintenance tents and pretending I knew what they should have been doing. I employed my old middle- and high-school teenage-boy immersion tactics, throwing footballs and rarely appearing in formfitting shirts. I taught martial arts, cracked jokes—the one about the goatfucker may have reappeared—and tried to ollie the skateboard a comm-school buddy had sent. I enjoyed it, of course, but also subconsciously knew this would make me look strong. I never discussed my romantic relationships, and only divulged personal information—number of brothers, age, hometown, undergrad major—with a calculating eye on how much vulnerability it would reveal, the less the better. Our staff NCOs told me, "You're one of the good lieutenants. You listen." Sure, I listened—I wanted to be liked, and I wanted no part of the way they treated Marla. Also, I was a second lieutenant, whereas my senior enlisted had eight to ten years of experience. I took most, if not all, of their suggestions, because they typically knew far more than I did. Because I was young, funny, and junior—and because I'd lucked into some smart, humane staff NCOs—this leadership style worked. I thought maybe I'd defied categorization as a bitch, dyke, or ho.

At the same time, as Marla chatted with the officers who came on to her, her posture and voice demure, I stewed with simultaneous feelings of superiority and envy. My belly peeked over my sagging trousers, and my cover molded my straight, short hair into instant hat-head. I was useless without my glasses. True, this androgynous armor—so similar to the flannel shirts and baggy jeans I'd worn in high school—shielded me from unwanted come-ons. No men so much as glanced my way, except to ask for extra radio batteries. Living up to the MIT stereotype, I was undatable, even surrounded by five thousand men in the desert. I wasn't consciously looking for love in Iraq—and since Marla was engaged, likely she wasn't, either. But her instinctive fem-

ininity and the attention it drew highlighted my embodiment
of its opposite. I figured I had two options: be like her and be
desired or be sexless and serious—but viewed as a legitimate
leader. Our troops respected me. But I felt like a failure at wom-
anhood, compared to her.

Marla cornered me one quiet afternoon outside the SYSCON,
a few months into our deployment. She held the last, worn
envelope from her fiancé. It had been nearly two months since
he'd written or emailed. Her calls had gone unanswered. Her
eyes teared up.

"He says he loves me, but—I don't know," she said.

"Sorry," I said. I didn't know how to respond. *Must be nice,*
I thought. *If it doesn't work out with the fiancé, you've got guys
lining up to take his place.*

"And the staff NCOs hate me. It's so hard to be a woman out
here," she said.

"Marla, no one hates you," I said. *Not every woman is like
you. Don't take me down with you.* It seemed as if she was trying to recruit me for a deployment cage match: Team Estrogen
versus Team Testosterone. But I identified with the men; I felt
like one of them. I thought we could all be one team.

"What about you? Are you okay with this?" she gestured
around our compound. "Don't you ever, like, put your insignia
in your ears to keep your ear piercings open? Or dance around
the shower trailer?"

What? No.

"I'm okay," I shrugged. I didn't want anyone to know how
not-okay I sometimes felt.

• • •

On April Fools' Day, we woke up to the news that sixteen miles
away, in Fallujah, four American contractors had been gunned
down and their burned bodies dragged through the streets,
then hung from a bridge. Days later, fifteen miles farther east,
three Marines in my college boyfriend Nathan's company died

from an IED hidden in a tree. A trip wire had been left hanging down; when the top of their Humvee ran into it, it detonated. At first, I wasn't sure if he was among them. It felt strange to wonder if the first guy I'd ever slept with had been blown to bits, both of us at war.

The following day, not near to our base but not too far from it either, a vehicle-borne IED hit a truck carrying troops. Jack, whose Mortuary Affairs bunker was a ten-minute stroll from the SYSCON, showed our company commander, a major, the bay of stretchers during "processing." In Iraq, caring for the dead took dramatically more effort than in civilian life. In this case, the body parts' contents needed sorting; remains from several Marines were mixed up, as if the gore had been scooped into bags in a hurry. For reasons no one could discern, the last body bag they opened contained all seven heads. The MA Marines painstakingly matched dog tags and personal effects to people. They marked the locations of wounds and tattoos on body-outline diagrams, shading in missing parts. Jack's platoon sergeant, Sergeant Mullins, helped supervise. In civilian life he'd been an ambulance driver, but even he hadn't seen things like this.

In that evening's formation, the major looked solemn. Then he told us we had to be more serious, to stop goofing off during slow moments, although we were on a base. I resolved to concentrate harder during my assigned watch, but at the same time, I wasn't sure how intensely one could fight in front of a computer monitor.

We called the dead "angels." In later years I would dismiss this nickname as mawkish crap, but there, on TQ, it fit. While the war continued outside the wire, base life was all telephone lines and plywood desks and trudges to the chow hall. The angels streamed through Mortuary Affairs in ones and twos. I stood SYSCON watch night after night, checked on my Marines in the afternoons.

No one anticipated Jack's story when he joined our lunch table the following week, on Good Friday, carrying limp cabbage on a plastic plate. He ate only salad and PowerBars now; soon his T-shirt would billow as he dropped more weight.

Today, Jack told us, there'd been a Marine who wasn't dead yet. He was mortally wounded, his heartbeat fading, and the doctors could do nothing more. They slung the Marine on a stretcher bound for MA. "Let us know when he stops breathing," they called to say every half hour, so they could fill out the death certificate. It was a weird arrangement, but Jack assented. What else could he have done? He wasn't a corpsman, and the docs needed to clear space for anyone else who might come through the trauma unit. He cued up *James Taylor's Greatest Hits*, Mortuary Affairs' now-standard playlist, something calming while they waited. The chaplain administered last rites. The Marines stalked away to wait; a few of them watched *Lord of the Rings*. Jack breathed along with the dying Marine and prayed. Years later, in a haze of prescription drugs, he would claim to have talked with him.

Finally the breathing stopped. The docs filled out the death certificate. Jack and his platoon cleaned and inspected the body, emptied pockets, inventoried personal effects. This one wasn't a KIA, killed in action, Jack said. This was a DOW, died of wounds. Soon I'd forget there was ever a time I didn't know those acronyms.

In chow-hall retellings, the episode became part of our Headquarters Battalion's lore. I thought too much about it, wrote it down, tried to make sense of it. I narrated it in an Easter email to my family, who wouldn't stop asking what was going on. This would shut them up.

Except it wouldn't. My mom's best friend forwarded it to twenty people. The next time I called home, my father said, "What a beautiful email. It made your aunt cry."

Christ, I thought. Deployment wasn't some movie playing eight thousand miles away, that you could cluck about Sunday in church before reclining in front of a Yankees game with a plate of nachos. My family wanted to sympathize, to reach me.

But it felt like they were exploiting the story to claim knowledge of something they didn't understand.

Technology made it easier to talk, but not to connect. My family thought they knew what I was going through when I emailed a photo or phoned on a staticky satellite line. But their stomachs weren't jolting when mortars exploded. They weren't confined to a few square miles of desert. They didn't smell the shitter trucks trailing sewage and disinfectant. They weren't walking my hamster Habitrail, an endless loop of chow-computers-wires-tent.

Or was I, in the retelling, exploiting Jack's story myself, sending home the catchiest tales in a bout of "no-shit-there-I-was"? Was I hamming it up, sending postcards on scraps of MRE boxes in a bid for authenticity, though I owned stationery? I wanted my well-meaning correspondents to respect my service, but not ask any questions. I was too tired and frustrated to elaborate further—and I didn't know how to respond.

Soon I stopped relaying anything sad. To fend off well-meaning inquiries, I wrote the World's Happiest War Blog, posting funny videos and making jokes about the enemy's bad aim. I uploaded a photo, all of Comm Company's officers together atop the SYSCON's roof. I stood in front, shoulder-height to everyone else. Marla, slim and willowy, stood next to me. My pistol showed outside my blouse, on my hip. A grainy printout of this would make it onto the corkboard of my old middle-school secretary's office. Learning this, I felt guilty, as if I didn't really deserve credit for going to war. I was only on a base, after all.

Marla, though, wanted to get as close as she could to the action. Unbeknownst to me—and our company's command—she'd started helping Jack. She'd been lukewarm about Comm Company's mission, but devoted herself to Mortuary Affairs, saying, "I just want to do more than sit on a FOB for six months while other Marines are fighting and getting killed." So she learned how to prep bodies. She went over to Mortuary Affairs' bunker every night, wore scrubs around, and carried a handheld radio when Jack went on convoys. She helped him write a binder full of standard operating procedures for his platoon. I saw their heads bent together over chow and wondered if Jack had a thing for her, too, like all the other guys out here seemed to.

She said he was training her so that if he got wounded or killed, she could take over Mortuary Affairs. "I'm actually making a difference," she told me, as if comm—for which many units depended on us—was meaningless. I understood her desire to get closer to the fight; most Marines wanted to serve at the tip of the spear, and Mortuary Affairs was about as close as one could get on our base. The platoon possessed a certain glamour—a holiness, even—because they cared for our version of martyrs: those killed in action.

Unlike Marla, I didn't want to stick out. Maybe this made me boring, but I wanted to do my assigned job—one I liked and was good at—using the brain for which I'd always been praised. Two months into deployment, I'd dialed in a robotic daily routine: SYSCON watch, workout, check on the Marines, report any issues, chow—and I tried to find fulfillment at the end of each day, when I prepped the network status report for our company's daily meeting.

Despite other officers' and staff NCOS' continued disagreements over how to lay fiber optic cable underground, the camaraderie felt thick at these evening meetings. We knocked on our plywood furniture to ensure luck from the gods of electronics. B-Ville took notes while sucking on a chicken-shaped, tamarind-flavored lollipop. Instructing Marines to keep track of equipment, Top would say things like, "You two touch dicks, and lemme eyefuck the plan before you get started," and no one would bat an eyelash. We had reason for cheer; we'd kept the network running while successfully transitioning the base's communications network from the army to the Marine Corps. I presented my reports confidently, with none of the internal stress that could roil during emotionally demanding one-on-

one meetings. Captain Davis and our company commander complimented my bearing and technical knowledge.

It took me weeks to realize I was the youngest person in our evening meetings, and (due to Marla's allotted sleep schedule) the only female. Not that I looked like one; I was more like everyone's little brother. It was like being part of a litter of foul-mouthed alpha puppies. Clive dispensed "combat noogies" when my helmet was off, and I wasn't quick enough to wriggle away from his Marlboro-fumed headlock. When Gunny Lars and I borrowed mitts and tossed a baseball, he asked if I'd "played some softball comin' up." Though I nodded that I had—I'd played on middle- and high-school teams—the real preparation had been in those backyard and schoolyard games with Dad and Danielle, where I'd learned that athletic performance would earn me approval. Later, horsing around, Captain Davis kicked my flak-jacketed chest. It didn't hurt, but the laws of physics were against me, and I flew backward, laughing. I'd grown up shoving and teasing my own brothers. In Comm Company, being the youngest, the smallest, and the most junior was an identity I gladly adopted; this way, they accepted me.

In mid-April after one of those meetings, our company commander leaned in and told us that we could expect a spike in network traffic in the coming week. I felt lucky that "increased network traffic" was our company's biggest professional worry. The infantry was about to attack Fallujah but would hold its fire for a day so Iraqi women, children, and elderly could escape. We had backup generators and topped-off fuel supplies, and we assumed the grunts would blast through the city. I wondered if we'd see the explosions from our base. *You can talk about us, but you can't talk without us*, we thought.

On the rumored invasion day, a few of us stood on top of the SYSCON, and my sergeants swore they saw splashes of fire. I squinted harder.

In the following five days, the infantry would invade Fallujah.

Nearly a month later, they would pull back to let the Iraqi "Fallujah Brigade" handle their own. By midsummer those Iraqis would dissolve into insurgent groups, necessitating the second battle of Fallujah that fall.

But at the moment, it didn't matter. Marines won't get off the roof when shit's blowing up.

SEVEN

Intrigue

Camp Taqaddum, Iraq—Deployment Day plus Two Months

One morning, I woke with a deep ache in my stomach. Fish had been an unwise choice for chow.

As I rolled out of my sleeping bag in green T-shirt and shorts, two navy nurses chatted in the corner of our tent, fifteen feet away. I knelt at the plastic bag tied to the corner of my cot, vomited yellow bile, and rested my head on the cot's taut surface. My stomach clenched; quietly, I threw up again, tied up the bag. I didn't want to draw attention; I just wanted to go to work and stand my watch. The nurses continued chatting. I pulled on camouflage trousers and blouse, put my pistol in its holster, pulled up thick socks and laced my boots. I slung my CamelBak over my shoulder, took a tentative sip of water, and carried the plastic bag outside before it leaked. As I walked toward the SYSCON, nausea rose again, compounded by bitter saliva. I tossed the bag in a trash can, run-walked to the head, leapt up the trailer steps and flung open a white stall door, then threw up into a low-flow toilet. I launched a couple more rounds before quieting. I wiped away the spit, washed my hands, and lurched to SYSCON.

Smiley Sam looked at me sideways. "Ma'am? You look pale."

I said, "Yeah, I'm not feeling so—" then darted aside to puke in a garbage bag full of MRE wrappers and coffee grounds.

Marla glided in, took one look at me, and offered to stand

the first few hours of my watch. The resentment I'd harbored towards her morphed into gratitude. Lightheaded, I stumbled back to my cot, where I barely unlaced my boots before falling into fitful sleep.

Hours later, I murmured awake. Someone shook my shoulder. I saw Smiley Sam's blurry outline above me. He handed me a large, silver bullet-shaped object. When I awoke the next morning—having been mercifully excused from my entire watch shift—I saw it was a container of thin Lipton soup. I thanked Sam in the SYSCON as he finished work. He replied, "That's not from me, ma'am. That's from Chief Warrant Officer Temple."

Jack. He'd had a tough couple of weeks: cutting down four burnt contractors from that bridge outside Fallujah, scraping human remains from a vehicle-borne IED, hauling bags full of feet and heads and guts. The infantry's aborted attack on the city made the casualties worse. Our company commander had told all of us officers to interact with Jack, cheer him up if possible, because his job was much harder than ours.

I unscrewed the thermos top and sniffed. Salty, with a chicken-onion tang. I could keep down small sips.

Later that day, during my few hours of freedom before the Comm Company meeting, I rinsed the thermos and crunched across the gravel to Jack's bunker. It was about a hundred yards from the chow hall and a quarter the size. Sandbags spelled "No One Left Behind" across its sloped roof. Despite recent battles ten miles away, the afternoon air felt peaceful; it had been a few days since we had been mortared.

I pushed open the heavy wooden door, greeted the corporal at the plywood desk, and peered around the corner to a makeshift room with "The Sir" wood-burned on a two-by-four above its threshold. Those Marines loved their chief warrant officer. Jack rose to his full six feet two and waved me in, smiling beneath his low brow. It was almost as if he'd been expecting me. He settled into his rolling desk chair and gestured to a black-padded office chair. I sat, handed him the thermos, and thanked him.

"Feeling better?" he asked. "Want a Pepsi?"

I nodded.

He swiveled his chair and reached into a camo-draped min-ifridge under his desk. Pepsi-can blue, the color of my prom dress, flashed as he passed the soda. I wiped the can's lip with a pinch of my shirt and sipped, waiting for my eyes to adjust to the dim light.

Looking to my left, I saw his platform bed, raised to store a footlocker underneath. A green canopy draped over his twin mattress. It was the first mattress I'd seen in two months; almost everyone on TQ slept in cots. Through the gauze, I could make out his sleeping bag, the lightweight "green mamba," topped by a poncho liner. A sweatshirt cased his pillow. He might have had a bed, but sheets were harder to come by. "Nice mosquito netting," I said.

Everything had been built from plywood and draped in olive drab. A shelf ran the length of wall behind the head of his bed and extended over a large janitor's sink, holding toothpaste, cocoa, and boxes of tea. I noticed a back door in the corner before my gaze looped back to Jack. To my right stood a gear tree: a three-foot-high crucifix stabilized by two-by-fours. His helmet rested atop the vertical post. The arms of the cross supported Jack's CamelBak and flak jacket, with blue-handled scissors taped into the jacket's webbing. His blood type was scrawled in black marker: O positive. We could give each other blood. A narrow bookshelf stood behind the gear tree, holding three-ring binders and a magnetic travel chess set.

Jack pointed to the chess set. "You play?"

"Badly," I said. "Even my baby brother kicks my ass." We traded more stories about his son, Sebastian, and my half brother, Zach.

Jack asked me what Zach wanted to be when he grows up. "I don't know," I said. "Last time I asked, it was a superhero or a fireman or a Teletubby. What does Sebastian want to be?"

"A Marine," Jack said, sighing. "I said he doesn't have to. I told him Daddy's been to war enough for everybody." His expression sobered. "I want my kid to be the biggest tie-dye-wearing, dope-smoking hippie he can be when he grows up."

I told him how Zach thought I was dead after seeing a TV news story involving four Marines killed in action. Jack said Sebastian worried about him, too. "But as long as he doesn't have to repeat third grade," he said, "he's smarter than his old man."

Over his shoulder, a computer screensaver blinked. I squinted to see a tan, blond kid cuddling a huge Great Dane.

"Is that him?" I asked.

"Yep, the son and the wife!"

I winced, looked down, weighed my Pepsi. Half of it left. Was he joking, or still married, or wasn't she dead? Anyway, it would be awkward to leave now.

"He's a handful," Jack went on. "Runs around, pain in the ass, mouths off. But he's a really great kid. So sometimes, you know, I just scare him. I go like *this*," Jack says, raising a backhand, "and he goes, *ungghh*." He shuddered.

You know, I thought.

I heard my stepdad's shout and saw my brother's nosebleed-soaked mattress.

I didn't ask how old Jack was when his dad stopped beating him. I just lifted my eyes to meet his. I wiggled the Pepsi-can tab until it twisted off in my fingers. Jack and I didn't speak, only looked at each other for a long minute.

Finally he smiled sadly. We talked of other things. He offered to lend me the book *Flags of Our Fathers*. I left with the creased paperback, glad he had spared me band-camp stories from "*last* year, the *real* war." I finished the book in one day and returned to drink tea and lose at chess the following night. At the end of the game, we fell silent, again held each other's eyes for too long.

• • •

Meanwhile, after two months of silence from her fiancé, Marla broke up with him. She soon gained the attention of a Cobra pilot: a dark-haired, attractive major whom we nicknamed "Major Glory." Before long, they were an item.

Marla kept trying to connect with me, to convince me to hang out, to be cool. She invited me to evening chow with her and Jack and Major Glory. I finally said I'd get coverage for an hour of watch. I got a little hungry in the SYSCON, anticipating a gristly burger, its spongy bun swiped with ketchup.

At the time we were all supposed to meet, Jack called the SYSCON.

"Marla's not here," I said.

He exhaled deeply and said, "I called to talk to you."

"You need a radio?"

"I, um, I feel like a high-school kid. I just wanted to say, I really wanted to go to dinner, but there's an angel coming in, and I have to be here."

"That's it?"

"Yeah. I'm really sorry."

"Dude. It's dinner. It'll happen again tomorrow. Neither of us is going anywhere out here."

The next afternoon, he knocked on the SYSCON door in full outside-the-wire kit, shoulder protectors flapping.

"Marla's not here," I said again, peeved. Male officers always barged in looking for Marla.

"I just came to tell you I'm leaving on a convoy in about an hour," he said. Convoys were dangerous in this area, prone to IEDs and small arms fire. Sometimes Marines didn't come back.

"You need something?" I asked. "Batteries? More handhelds? Should Marla get down to MA?"

"No, I just wanted to tell you I'm leaving on a convoy."

"I'll tell Marla. You sure you don't need anything?"

"I'm sure," he said softly.

"Well, good luck," I said. "See you later."

He clomped off. I checked the networks, made my reports to our higher command. I told Marla when I saw her, in case she needed to check in on the MA Marines. In case Jack's visit had been some sort of signal between them.

A few nights later, we all went to chow—her, Major Glory, Jack, and me. Lobster night beckoned, in all its fluorescent-lit furor. The chow hall echoed with slamming trays and shouted conversations: *Gonna eat that?—Fuck yeah, hands off!—HALO tournament—Hot sauce, dickwad—A son! I got cigars!—I got a cigar for ya . . .*

I shuffled to the seat Marla had saved and picked at my lobster tail, digging out slivers of white meat, breaking tines off the cheap plastic fork. I scraped as much as possible into a mound on my plate, poured on liquid fake-butter, then ate the mix.

Jack sat next to me. He leaned over close so his temple grazed mine. "Can I show you something?" he asked. "Give me your fork." On his lobster, he showed me how to liberate the green tendril of intestine from the rest of the carcass. "You've been mixing that in there all this time," he said. Marla giggled. I slouched as my appetite disappeared. I didn't know not to eat the green stuff.

"Oh," I said, my face burning. *Can't even solve this lame-ass deployment's First World problems.*

Major Glory glanced sideways at Marla. *Probably thinking about getting laid*, I thought, irritated by their closeness and laughter. I sensed Jack was jealous of him; when Marla said something about the presidential election, he called her a crazy bitch.

She ignored him, stood up, and sauntered away with Major Glory to select a dessert. "Hey," I said, in a loud whisper, "you sound like a dick." I wondered again if he had a thing for Marla, like half the other men seemed to. But Jack apologized. "A little punchy," he said. "Long night."

In the following weeks, Comm Company thinned out its personnel. A third of the Marines got to fly home early, since the bulk of the base setup was done. Our company commander disappeared, along with several others. Marla, me, and Captain Davis—frocked to Major Davis, because he now doubled

as our company commander and battalion executive officer—
were the only commissioned officers left in our company. Chief
Warrant Officer Clive remained, too, as the operations officer.
Around this time, Major Davis learned of Marla's nights helping out with Mortuary Affairs. Marla thought about the bodies afterward—it was fucking her up a little, she said, but she'd
much rather do this than comm. Privately, she sneered at our job
in the SYSCON, said we were just sitting there, that taking care
of our brothers in arms in the way that she did mattered more.

And in some ways, yes, it did matter more. Our warrior ethos
glorified anything close to the fight, and comm was downright
antiseptic next to cleaning dead bodies. Marla told me about
the latest casualties, two Marines who drowned during a river
patrol in the Euphrates. One had a head injury; one didn't. They
surmised the second had gone in after his buddy. Their gear's
weight drowned them. She described their distended lips and
swollen bodies.

I was fascinated, but the gruesomeness put me off. Unlike
Marla, I actually liked my assigned job. Maybe this made me
less hardcore—but I was good at comm, thought I contributed,
and thought our unit helped others. I only occasionally judged
myself for wielding electrons instead of a rifle.

Soon Major Davis forbade Marla from further performing
mortuary affairs duties, no matter how personally fulfilling her
experience was. With so few officers in the company, he said,
we had to stick to our assigned mission. Marla argued that she
was showing initiative, but in the end she couldn't fight it. He
was our boss. And we had a job to do.

Despite this changed arrangement, and the prickliness
between them at chow, Jack and Marla remained friends. He
joked to her that he'd "put the moves" on me. She repeated the
joke in the SYSCON one afternoon, unpacking Nutella from her
mother's care package.

I said, "The way he talks, I thought his wife was dead, or
they're divorced!"

"Nope, very much alive. And he talks a big game, but they're still married," Marla said.

Gunny Duncan, the multichannel radio staff NCO, overheard us. The Marines all considered him a father figure and revered his technical expertise. "Ma'am, Chief Warrant Officer Temple is *old*. Also, he's married! We know there ain't no way that's gonna happen," he said. The staff NCOs respected me and thought me responsible—certainly not marriage-threateningly attractive.

The Iraqis thought me feminine, though. A couple of the men who worked in the base's tiny restaurant were friendly. Borderline creepy. They were from Babylon, south of TQ. The one manning the chicken counter asked my name. When I pointed to my nametape and said, "Lieutenant Fazio," he mimicked, "tfazio." I shrugged okay. And though I could not pronounce his name, he was persistent. He taught me "shukran"—thank you; and "eliom"—today; and "maku moshkine"—no problem. He printed the Arabic words in my journal in precise mechanical pencil. For many months, shukran was the only word I remembered. I would say it after ordering chicken shawarma, then quickly step away from the counter to discourage further conversation.

Why so quick to disengage? Because the first time I thanked the counter guy for my chicken, he said, "You're welcome, tfazio; I love you, tfazio. You have boyfriend? You have husband?" I claimed a boyfriend back in the States and escaped with my meal.

Another afternoon I stretched before a run, pistol in one hand, loaded magazine in the other. My weapon and ammo went everywhere I did. Eighty-degree sunshine bathed my pasty legs. I wore standard Marine PT gear—olive-green T-shirt and running shorts.

I heard a rumble, and two truckloads of Iraqi workers drove by, cheering wildly. Confused, I waved back. They cheered even louder, raising arms and whirling head scarves. I waved again, this time with my pistol hand. *Motherfuckers*, I thought. But I managed a half smile. I'd come halfway around the world to be catcalled for the first time. It wasn't the last attention from them I got.

One night I sat in the Iraqis' tea garden in 0100 starlight, writing a letter to my brother Matt. We'd been in the same Boston ROTC consortium. Three years prior, he'd returned from summer training and pressed a small curl of dusky silver into my palm. Jump wings.

"If you keep them safe, I'll always be safe," he'd said.

He'd tagged along on field exercises with Marine midshipmen, sailing through grueling hikes and rappelling down university buildings. At my commissioning, Matt and our brother Dave had pinned second lieutenant bars on my shoulders. Matt was now a senior air force cadet and would graduate soon. The distance between Boston and Iraq seemed interplanetary.

I heard a rustle behind me: the thin-mustached waiter who manned the counter. He set a silver tray before me, brown tea in a shot glass embraced by a thin metal holder, tiny dish of brown sugar lumps beside it. I told him no thanks, I didn't want it, but he just said, "It is you."

"Hey—" I tried to protest, but he ignored me, repeated, "It is you," then walked away. I called meekly after him, "Shukran." Thank you.

I moved the tray to the next table over, not touching a drop. Some gifts, I was bad at accepting.

• • •

Soon the Iraqis' familiarity was the least of my worries. One afternoon while I showered, Marla burst into the trailer. There was an emergency, she said, and I was needed at the SYSCON. I hustled there in shorts and T-shirt, still in flip-flops, holding my wet purple towel. The company first sergeant, Marla, and our three female enlisted Marines—two corporals and a PFC— waited there.

A female Marine in another unit had been raped behind the heads near our compound late last night, the balding first sergeant told us. A male in T-shirt and sweatpants had held a pistol to her head. Marla looked grave. Pissed off, I vowed after sundown I'd keep a round in my nine-mil's chamber. I jabbered indignantly about force protection, about martial arts, about grab-twist-pull. That last comment elicited a laugh from our enlisted women, who remained otherwise stoic and composed. Later I'd wonder how often they'd seen this scenario.

The first sergeant calmed me down, said we were the first ones he'd told, and that Marla and I should brief the rest of our Marines. We were, after all, the platoon commanders.

After I returned to my tent and dressed, I gathered up my two platoons—men in their teens and twenties, plus my one female corporal—in front of the maintenance bay. Some of the more rambunctious Marines—my favorites—fidgeted in the back of the cluster. Somehow between the six-mile endurance course, remedial land navigation, and being an audience for long-forgotten Pentagon wags, there had been no training module in Quantico for Talking To Nineteen-Year-Olds About Rape.

Haltingly, I explained the situation. Spitting out the words out felt surreal. I had never before said "rape" out loud.

"Any questions?" I asked, praying for none. But one Marine in the back raised his hand.

"Ma'am, how do we know she's telling the truth?"

I was aghast. I said what the first sergeant had told me—the docs used a rape kit to examine her, and the results bore it out. It hadn't occurred to me that anyone would lie about something like this. "You know, in a crime like this, things, uh—happen to, uh—people's bodies," I stammered. "NCIS is investigating everything. They said it was true."

I then briefed them on the base's newest rule—all Marines had to use the buddy system after dark. I tried to emphasize that it was for force protection. That there was a criminal running loose—and don't forget about the insurgents, we were at war—and that we all had to look out for each other. That on a different base, there had been a third-country national lurking in the female showers. Finally I ended with a warning not to pet the wildlife. The Marines masked their smirks so I could end platoon commander's time and rub my aching temples. Fuck. I wanted Advil. And bourbon.

We got no more news after that, neither of the rape nor its victim nor its perpetrator. I doubted NCIS would ever apprehend anyone, since our base saw plenty of convoy and air traffic every day. The rapist could have come and gone several times in the day it took for word to spread.

Three weeks later, rumors swirled about a different rape. The talk put me on edge, highlighting these assaults as just another fucked-up fact of deployed life. But no sooner did the allegations become public than the female Marine confessed it was fraudulent, a lie told to hide an affair resulting in a pregnancy. *Seriously? Who does this shit?* I thought.

Now I knew why my Marines had been skeptical of the first one. I wish they hadn't hardened themselves in this way, to be so desensitized to a crime that their first response was to question the woman's integrity. Their reaction frustrated me. But I was also ashamed of my gender.

Regardless of the facts surrounding either incident, the new orders stayed in place: anyone walking after dark had to have a "battle buddy." Jack volunteered to walk me back from SYSCON watch. When I finished at 2300, his six feet filled the doorframe.

"If you're not tired, we can sit in the tea garden," he said the first night. I was not tired. An Arabic remix of "Dancing Queen" whined in the background. Jack produced a magnetic travel chess set from his pocket. We faced off in white plastic chairs reminiscent of patio furniture, the beach without the ocean, two new friends, pistols at our hips. A scraggly, brittle-leaved tree hung over us, its scarred trunk bearing a sheen of dust. As moonlight slanted, I contemplated my first move.

I bopped my head to the faint pulsing music; only our distance from the market's subwoofers kept us safe from thumping bass and wailing melody. I squinted to discern the pieces in the dim light.

It didn't matter whether I picked white or black; Jack beat me in chess. Children had bested me before, and he was no tyro. Under his gaze, I felt like a plastic pawn with a tiny magnetic bottom. My concentration, though, was anything but magnetic. With our heads bent together, my thoughts inched forward as my pieces plodded, square by square. He deciphered my clumsy plans for next moves. He, on the other hand, calculated precise traps, fondling bishops into place.

That night I could still tell white from black, right from wrong.

• • •

The following morning, I made good on my promise to increase force protection in the wake of the rape. I taught the Marine Corps Martial Arts Program, which bundled aikido, jiu-jitsu, and judo techniques with more traditional hand-to-hand combat training: bayonet thrusts and parries, knife fighting, chokes, and handy tutorials on killing someone with a shovel. I had attained "green-belt-instructor" level back at Quantico, which involved lots of crawling through mud, falling on the ground, and feigning motivation. This qualified me to run courses on TQ.

We started class at 0630 and practiced break falls in the sand. Shards of concrete slapped our elbows, which cracked, bled, scabbed, and slimed over with sweat. Then the scabs would rip off, and they'd bleed all over again. Our knuckles bled, too, after punching black pads. I couldn't clench a fist without trickling plasma. When we hip-threw each other in the dirt, grit collected in our underwear. I shook sand from my sports bra before every shower.

My Marines badly needed this training. Not necessarily because they'd engage the enemy in hand-to-hand combat—the recent rape aside, attacks on the base were at that point rare—but precisely because they *wouldn't* do this. Martial arts practice made my computer-repairing troops feel tough, like real

Marines. It helped them blow off steam after long days, keeping them out of trouble. Advancing in belt level also increased their scores for promotion in rank. We couldn't control the jobs we were assigned, but we could control how aggressive we made ourselves when doing them.

One popular drill, named "bull-in-the-ring," involved one Marine in the center of a circle—the "bull." Others came up to fight him one by one. The bull had to ward them all off using countering moves. I demonstrated "counter to the front bear hug," where an opponent hugs around your arms, and you have to break free. In the middle of the ring, a larger Marine (who had me by about a foot and at least 40 pounds) swept his arms out to bear-hug me but missed completely. He barely caught the top of my head. I looked up at him and blinked.

We renamed that "counter to the front air hug."

A tall, camo-clad form materialized on the outskirts of the bull-in-the-ring. It was Jack, watching me teach. When I yelled hello, he lifted his blouse to show his black belt. As a black belt instructor, he could take over the class if he wanted to. But he asked me first, standing at a respectful distance, before coaching one of my Marines on a technique.

That night, over chess in the tea garden, he said, "You're a great teacher, a natural in front of a crowd." He told me about the Gracie Fighting Academy in Brazil, where the crowning highlight of his martial arts achievement wasn't the black belt course through which the Marines had sent him, but his chance to "roll with the old man," a senior instructor at Gracie. The wiry septuagenarian had beaten Jack in seconds. I listened, digesting his compliment. He didn't know that I felt bashful in front of the troops in my own martial arts class. I tried to make my tea last awhile, gulping the final sweet thimbleful when I couldn't hold my pee anymore, and it was time to go.

As we left the tea garden, Jack invited me to watch a movie that Friday night. I paused a few beats; did this mean something more? Though he'd been my sole battle buddy those past several nights, I'd thought maybe he was just being friendly. I wondered if anyone—his Marines, my Marines, our company officers—would notice if I went to his bunker again, alone. If they noticed, would I still be respected?

Looking back, it seems naïve, but I said yes.

On "movie night," I walked into Jack's bunker, made a right toward his room, and sat in the same office chair as before. He cued up his laptop and secured his door with a thick shard of pine. I raised an eyebrow as he slid the lock. Privacy was a privilege; almost no one on TQ had doors, let alone ones that locked. Most of us just had tent flaps. "So the Marines know not to bother us," he said. I trusted him.

We picked at random from a binder of scratched DVDs, coming up with a bootleg copy of Jack Black and Ben Stiller's *Envy*. My leg bounced with nerves. By the middle of the movie, Jack and I stole glances at each other when each of us thought the other wasn't looking. As the end neared, the DVD hemorrhaged in digital failure. Jack Black remained a smattering of pixels. We couldn't get it to play again, and shrugged defeat. But I didn't want to call the evening over, and it seemed Jack didn't, either. He flipped on his radio to the Armed Forces Network, the only station that worked. We chatted—even now, I can't remember what about—only that he draped his arm over his chair's armrest and looked me in the eyes, dangling his meaty hand as if daring me to take hold.

A Liz Phair melody drifted from the radio. That I do remember.

Why can't I breathe whenever I think about you?

Jack stared at me, then leaned forward, lifted a hand, and tucked a stray hair behind my ear. "I find you very attractive," he said.

Jack was thirteen years my senior, married, a father. I'd never been hit on by someone no longer a boy.

He took my hand, tried to pull me up out of my chair.

"Aren't you technically still married?" I said.

He admitted he was. We paused for what seemed like eternity. "Come on," he said. "I'll walk you home." We walked in silence and traded awkward, perfunctory good-byes as I ducked through my tent flap. He was married. He had a kid. I figured of course things were bound to get intense here, on deployment, with all the bullshit our jobs entailed. His especially, wading through guts. But to do anything about it would be dishonorable. And for us—for Marines in a war—honor had value. At least I wanted it to.

· · ·

Two mornings later, Marla and I were both due to be promoted to first lieutenant, which only required two years in service and a pulse. As we formed up for the ceremony, I saw Jack lingering in the back row, along with other officers from my company.

Clive read the promotion proclamation. Apparently the president of the United States was "reposing special trust and confidence" in Marla and me. Major Davis swore us in, and Staff Sergeant Garcia and Gunny Lars pinned matte black first lieutenant bars to my collar. Despite our frustrations and the ass-chewings I'd gotten from Major Davis, I respected these men immensely, and felt relieved that they seemed proud of me. All the while I could feel Jack's green eyes at the back of the formation, smiling at parade rest, focused on the back of my neck. Special trust and confidence. I must not fuck this up.

Meanwhile, Major Glory, Marla's pilot boyfriend, came to the front of the formation and pinned on her first lieutenant bars. After the ceremony, she whispered to me that he'd organized a wetdown for us. Traditionally when officers are promoted, they spend the difference in paycheck on alcohol for everyone they know. Alcohol was prohibited for us in a combat zone.

But it seemed as if on TQ, alcohol was tolerated if it was kept quiet. Some officers and staff NCOs got bottles of "Listerine" sent to them. If any junior Marine was found with it, though, they got in trouble.

I wanted to do my damnedest to lead by example; though I was confused about Jack, I could at least do this one thing right. I figured there should be at least one sober officer in the company, in case the generators broke or we got mortared—and both happened too often for my taste. I had always been the dorky rule-follower. "Special trust and confidence," I thought again. The no-alcohol rule, I'd obey. I didn't go to the wetdown.

But Marla pressured me to socialize, to hang out with her pilot friends when I'd rather have hidden. Her visits to their tent were risky. Being seen in public as Major Glory's girlfriend— approaching him with doe eyes and casual affection, having him pin her at her promotion—undermined her credibility. This was a clear double standard, of course. No one judged Major Glory for dating her—in fact, he likely got high-fived—but Marla was perceived as unprofessional. The rumor mill churned quickly on deployment, and details didn't matter; perceptions did. I didn't want to risk being viewed as anything other than a solid Marine.

For example, a story had made the rounds about another female lieutenant and male pilot. They were dating; maybe they were even married. At least neither Marla nor I had heard that either of them was married to anyone else. They might have been on Al Asad, the other big air base, or it might have happened in Baghdad. She might have even been army instead of Marine. The female lieutenant had her own room, similar to the one-story concrete hut Marla now slept in; it was a room I refused to share with her because I thought she and Major Glory might do things like this. One day the young female lieutenant— midtwenties or so—and the slightly older male pilot—maybe thirty, but not yet gone to dad-bod—filed into that room. An enlisted Marine, or maybe a few, had seen them go in together. At least one of them crept to the window; if it had blinds, there must have been some gaps. And although smartphones did not yet exist, and though his M16 must have been unwieldy, the culprit who'd crept to the window possessed a camera that let him shoot video.

The young female lieutenant didn't find out right away. A few mornings later, her harried boss—a major, I think, perhaps not so different from our major—called her into his makeshift office. He might have pressed his thumb and forefinger to the bridge of his nose. There was a file on the shared drive he wanted her to explain. He clicked his mouse a few times, motioned her to look at his monitor. There, in all of its Quicktime glory: the young lieutenant and her pilot boyfriend, fucking.

She was offered a transfer back stateside. But she wanted to serve in Iraq, didn't want to let this stop her, even though most of her battalion had by now seen the video. Her courage was striking. But I didn't want that to be me.

So I stayed on guard the next time Marla convinced me to take an extended dinner break with her, Major Glory, and his friend Tim, a six-foot-five helicopter pilot. Tim spoke with a slight country accent, was outgoing and enthusiastic. When he bent at the waist to shake my hand, I felt like half a circus act. Months later, I would find out that his wife and three-year-old daughter lived back in the Ozarks, but Marla did not know this. Instead she thought she was doing me a favor; she was trying to set me up. I made awkward conversation at the chow hall, repeating to myself: *It's nice to socialize. It's nice to socialize. Goddamn I hate meeting new people.*

Twilight descended, the air cooled, and after dinner we walked to the tea garden. We met up with two female officers from battalion headquarters. One, a logistician, described how she'd gone with a few senior officers for lunch at a local sheik's compound. The sheik had cut her meat for her, complimenting her beauty. Soon he was talking to the battalion leadership about money, gesturing her way, asking if she had a husband. She was a prior-enlisted first lieutenant, a mother of two going through a divorce, and told the story with alternating outrage and amusement. The running joke among the battalion officers thereafter—which may not have been a joke at all—was that the sheik had tried to negotiate for her hand in marriage.

I raised my eyebrows in polite incredulity, squirming. I shrank from discussions of sexism, either ours or the Iraqis', and I didn't hang out with many other female officers. Part of this was due to our shifting schedules and our small numbers. But in retrospect, I was also trying not to appear part of a feminine cabal. Away from other women, I could blend more easily into the desert-camo mass of Marines and conform to the default-male behaviors around me. I didn't like being singled out as female, and hanging out with other women made that more likely.

Soon an entourage of male pilots joined us around the cigarette-burnt picnic table. Marla had invited them. It was clear the pilots thought they'd hit the jackpot. The night resembled a wardroom officer's call, or an evening at Pizza Port back in Carlsbad. We lifted sodas to sunburnt lips, tore Frisbee-sized discs of chewy flatbread, and traded stories from the Basic School. The pilots were flirty with the other lieutenants, but the women rebuffed them. I kept quiet. After an hour, I shook the last drop from my Coke and excused myself to return to the SYSCON.

Tim, the helicopter pilot, walked me back to Comm Company's compound. He bowed again to shake my hand and said he enjoyed my company. I thanked him but turned away. I didn't trust his motives and didn't want to be seen with him alone. I resented Marla for inviting me out.

Why did I not confide in her about Jack's advances, as she'd confided in me about Major Glory and her former fiancé? Though such intimacy is often the bedrock of female friendship, in my mind, gossiping about crushes made me unacceptably vulnerable, even weak. If other Marines perceived me as too close to Marla, I figured I'd lose their respect. And if she couldn't keep her own secrets, how could I be sure she'd keep mine? It would be several years before I learned that expressing feelings openly was the key to attracting romance. But Iraq was a tough place to implement that. In light of our stoic warrior ethos, I didn't want my male colleagues to learn—even secondhand—that I felt anything at all.

Jack was only person with whom I felt comfortable sharing emotion. We continued to see each other under the guise of friendship, continuing our late-night chess matches under our usual tree. On a night when I was bruised and tired from martial arts, we sipped tea and went through the motions of moving our pieces. Within minutes, we gave up the game. We talked about home a little; we stared at each other a lot. He didn't sleep much, and he'd lost weight. It had been a hard day in Comm Company, too; the fiber wasn't getting buried underground fast enough; the Marines were tired; crucial spare parts for the trenching tools had to be flown in from the States.

"I bet Clive's intimidated by you," Jack said.

I snorted. "Me? He's been around for a billion years. I don't even know what I'm doing."

We caught whiffs of cigarette smoke drifting from other tables. I pretended to look at the chessboard, tried to find the groove in the tea garden's music. I didn't know then that most butterbars felt as I did: ravenous for empathy and approval, but loath to admit it.

"I think you're doin' just fine," Jack said.

I felt a fierce wave of homesickness burn and exhaled, slouching back in my chair.

"I miss my brothers," I said, looking skyward. Jack leaned an elbow on the armrest of his cracked plastic chair, dipped his head to peer at me.

"I'm sorry you're sad," he said. "But you are . . ." he paused, sighed. "Loved."

EIGHT

Past and Future

A few weeks after my promotion, I tore off to Jack's bunker with a package from my brother Matt. "Look, he sent me his cover!" Matt had recently graduated from college and ROTC. I'd planned to be in Boston to swear him in, but deployment had gotten in the way. Since I couldn't pin on his insignia in person, he'd sent me his uniform cap on which to fasten his shiny gold butterbar. The cap was a blue "pisscutter," shaped like a fast-food employee would wear. I pinned the bar through the fabric and slipped two of my matte-bronze lieutenant bars into the return envelope. Before sealing the package, I whispered, "If you deploy and die, I'll kill you."

Jack listened to me go on about Matt—how proud I was.

"My dad beat the shit outta me till I was thirteen," he said.

I asked him what happened then.

"My folks split up. I stayed with my mom. She didn't want me for long."

He looked at his screensaver; it'd flipped to Sebastian on a playground. "As a parent, how could you say that?" he said. "How could you not want your kid?"

Jack got into his share of trouble in high school, couldn't see the point of staying when he could work for money. After ninth grade, he got a job busing tables in a mom-and-pop restaurant.

The Italian couple screamed at each other all the time. But they were nice to him, fed him, let him sleep in a lean-to out back. After a few months of that, the Marine Corps recruiter got hold of him. Jack just wanted to get the hell out of his hometown. In the space of an afternoon, the recruiter became both his high-school principal and his mother.

When he became a recruiter himself, he realized how illegal it'd been for the recruiter to forge those signatures. But Jack had joined up in the '80s; back then, no one had cared. And he loved being a devil dog. Even now, eighteen years later, he didn't know what else he'd do, if he couldn't do this anymore. Live on his boat, he figured.

Combined with the powerful accelerant of potential mortars and convoys, these stories made each hour with Jack seem as if I'd known him a year. Knowing his past felt like secret power; soon I thought we could read each other's minds.

In the following weeks, I found an excuse to hang out in his office every couple of days. He worried aloud about his Marines and felt guilty for signing up his platoon—originally a chemical weapons-detection unit—to pick up chunks of dismembered humans. He talked about the angels he could not get out of his mind: the dead lieutenant with an ultrasound of his unborn child in his pocket. Jack hated being away from his own son, his reason for living.

Maybe if I stayed and listened, I could relieve some of his burden. But it wasn't quite that—I am not that much of an altruist. I thought perhaps if I stayed long enough, some of his work would rub off on me. I'd be close to something important— might, by proxy, do enough to be worthy of saying I contributed to this war.

And maybe if I listened hard, Jack would love me and want to stay with me. If he did—and if I became Sebastian's stepmom—I thought I could fix his broken family better than I ever knew how to fix mine.

I kept going to Jack's bunker. He told me more stories.

He had marched through boot camp and drove armored vehicles and had been left drunk and naked in McDonald's by his buddies, all before I could hook a bra behind my back.

He told me he'd been stationed out west when he met his wife. She was a local girl. He was maybe twenty-two. I was in fifth grade. He'd fallen in love with her family: a doting mother, a father he respected, parents he'd never had. He'd married her secretly in Vegas before he deployed to the first Gulf War. While he was gone, her mother asked if they planned to get married. His young bride let slip that they already were.

When Jack returned from Kuwait, he had doubts, he said. But his wife and mother-in-law had already planned a big reception. And he did, for the first time, finally feel like he had a family.

Their son was born the summer I got my learner's permit. A few years later, Jack deployed to a training exercise in Thailand, on a boat that stocked extra antibiotics for Marines whoring in Bangkok. Even the chaplain got a lap dance. But not Jack. He thought he was the only faithful devil dog, he said. Then he got home and found a letter.

A love letter addressed to his wife. It wasn't from him.

I thought back to a winter morning in second grade, when Matt, Dave, and I had awoken to shouting. In my pajamas, I ran toward the argument; my brothers stayed behind in their room. Our carpeted hallway seemed endless. Before I reached the kitchen, I heard Dad shout, "What is this?" Though it was loud, it sounded as though he could barely say the words.

I stopped in the hall. The sun was up, but not by much. The only light-glow came from the kitchen.

I heard Mom's choked and garbled whimper. "What is this?" Dad said again.

He stalked by me, down the hall, and called us kids into the boys' room. We three sat on a twin bed, still rumpled from sleep. "Children, Mommy cheated on me," Dad said. "We're getting a divorce."

When Matt had asked, "What's cheating?" Dad only replied, "She slept with another man."

I told Jack none of this as he sighed and looked straight at me. "Up until then, I thought that if any woman ever cheated on me, I would just leave," he said. "Then I looked at my three-year-old. And there was no way that kid was growing up without a father."

I hustled out of Jack's room with a quickness that afternoon.

• • •

In those months, James Taylor still played while the mortuary affairs Marines worked on the bodies. Every morning when I woke, "Fire and Rain" beat chords in my skull. *Just got to see me through another day.*

Early one evening in June, I pushed open Jack's bunker door. On the concrete floor lay a single aluminum transport case, different from the others I'd seen. This one contained a body bag. I watched as Marines draped the Stars and Stripes over it and tied the flag tight with twine.

Jack came around a corner, shoulders muscled under thin scrubs. A sad smile spread across his scruffy cheeks.

There weren't enough troops to man the six handles rimming the case's perimeter. Standing by a handle, I saw my chance. I genuflected, "here, I'll help—" and the case was heavier than I expected. My cover tumbled to the deck.

Together we lifted the transport case. I almost puked. *This confirms it,* I thought. *I don't have the cojones for war.*

We carried the case to the warped plywood door counterweighted with a sand-filled plastic bottle. We whacked our shins on the doorjamb and cursed over the threshold; a Humvee idled outside. The door banged behind us.

We laid the transport case behind the vehicle, sweating in hot night wind. While a sergeant pulled down the Humvee's tailgate, Laredo, a sinewy lance corporal about my height, materialized behind my left shoulder. He said quietly, "Ma'am, will you hold my clipboard?"

I glanced back. "Sure," and turned around.

As he handed me the clipboard, he switched places with me, taking his rightful position in front of the transport case handle. His rope-veined forearms flexed, and six Marines lifted in practiced unison. The transport case continued its journey onto the airfield, away from Taqaddum, to Al Asad, Landstuhl, Dover. Its weight stayed in my wrists.

I felt as if I had helped for once, at least a little. Must have been the same reason Marla had wanted to do this so badly.

After the Humvee left, Jack's Marines flitted around clean stretchers, laying out new supplies. I followed him back to his room. We said nothing; circles sagged under his eyes. I couldn't tell if he blinked back tears or exhaustion. With his left hand, he took my right. Our fingers curled into each other's, yin and yang.

• • •

In the following weeks, a nineteen-year-old PFC killed himself with his M16. Jack said the suicide note began, "Yesterday I forgot to shave. This is bad. The other day I was late to formation. This is very bad."

NCIS had to examine the body before Mortuary Affairs could do its work. Jack stayed up late, waiting for the go-ahead. Though I'd later be ashamed of it, my first reaction at this news was not sorrow for the young Marine, but anger and frustration that I couldn't hang out with Jack because he had to work. It was our deployment's first suicide. It wouldn't be the last.

Our "movie night" repeated on the nights there were no casualties. Next chance we got, we watched *Enemy at the Gates*. Though the plot involved Rachel Weisz and Jude Law having sex inches from their comrades, Jack and I remained mostly chaste. He extended his arm my way, stroking my hair and hands. When he pulled me up to stand against him, I did not stop him. I finally let him hug me.

I clasped my hands behind him, feeling the faint flash of fat on his hips, which would disappear as his appetite deserted him. His hands roamed my ribcage, then settled at the small of my back, where his fingers traced circles. I nosed the notch of his V-necked scrub shirt, felt his chest fuzz, heard his pulse pound beneath a jiu-jitsu tattoo. The lowest ribs on his right side thickened into bony knots. I kneaded them with my fingers. Neither of us knew when a trilling phone or hauled stretcher would throw the evening into crisis. A plywood door slammed somewhere else in the bunker. I jolted away. Surprise flashed across Jack's face, then sad resignation.

"Come on," he said. "I'll walk you home."

As we walked to my tent, gravel underfoot changed to smooth dirt, then concrete. My stomach clawed. As we neared my tent, I said, "So, tomorrow?"

I suspected everyone in a ten-tent radius could hear us. Actually, I suspected everyone on the planet could hear us.

He said, "I have to limit the amount of time I spend with you."

"Oh," I said.

He said, "I am—I have—completely fallen for you."

The tendrils in my stomach turned into a lightning sear. "Okay," was all I said.

He called, "good night," as I stumbled through my tent flap. Without thinking further, I shucked my wet undershorts, kicked into my sleeping bag, and abandoned the complications of consciousness.

The next morning, the memory of Jack's hug seemed surreal. I shook out a fresh pair of socks. *I've needed a hug since I got to Iraq*, I thought. Half the time, I felt an ecstasy of love and purpose; the connection felt like emotional crack. At the same time, I wanted to preserve my reputation as the smart little lieutenant, the good kid, and do the right thing. Clearly Iraq was the least convenient possible place to have a romantic awakening. Jack and I walked a fine line, but we hadn't crossed any legal boundaries. Adultery had to be penetrative sex, according to

the Uniform Code of Military Justice. To be prosecuted, it had
to be substantiated by a confession or an eyewitness. What I'd
done wasn't smart, but at least it wasn't illegal.

In my journal, I jotted lines from *The Love Song of J. Alfred
Prufrock*:

> Do I Dare
> Disturb the Universe?
> In a minute there is time
> For decisions and revisions which a minute will reverse

I walked to the SYSCON, stuffing down my guilt long enough
to savor the memory of Jack holding me. He'd said he loved
me. After the weeks of deaths, I had to believe in something,
even if I knew it was wrong. Even if later, it would hurt like a
motherfucker.

I also knew I should hide how I felt in front of everyone else.

At my desk, I scrolled through a few pictures until I found
the one I wanted. I changed my laptop background to a snap-
shot from the day of Matt's commissioning: Matt, Dave, Dad,
and Grandpa posed for the camera in front of an oil painting.
Each of them looked stern. Watching me. Judging. It was a
reminder of everything I'd learned as a kid: stay invisible. Don't
shame the family.

• • •

I walked with Marla and Jack to noon chow that day. Jack's eyes
danced, but we said nothing we couldn't say in front of anyone
else. He and Marla had grown apart since she'd started dating
Major Glory and been barred from helping Mortuary Affairs. I'd
told her nothing of my visits to his bunker. As we stood in line
to wash our hands, Jack said to us both, "well, I finally wrote a
letter last night telling Medusa it's over." My head snapped up.
Medusa was his mean nickname for his wife. But out loud, in
plain daylight, did this mean he was ending his marriage?

"Wow," Marla murmured.

"Yeah, and then I told the combat stress doc today," Jack continued. "She said, 'You don't do *anything* like that when you're over here. Don't make any decisions in this place.'" My hopes sank. Was this instead a coded message telling me he *wasn't* leaving her? Or would he wait to get back home before divorcing his wife?

Confused, I let the conversation flow on to other things.

What had happened in Jack's bunker had to stay just between him and me. If I told Marla, she might gossip about me or entrust me with worse secrets in return. I didn't want to suffer the same penalties she faced for appearing—let alone actually being—sexually available. Not that anyone paid attention to me in that way; Clive and my gunny and staff sergeants certainly didn't. Our conversations centered only on whether we could lay fiber optic cable underground fast enough. If anyone—especially Major Davis—found out about Jack and me, it would wreck my credibility.

I did not then know how many junior officers also felt they walked the same tightrope over an abyss of imminent failure, whether in romance, work, or family life. The Marine Corps' high standards only lessened the margin for error. I just thought if I flagellated myself enough, I could stay ahead of criticism. And soon I would go back to Jack's room, looking for an escape.

So, when he emailed me a quantum physics question he'd pulled off the internet, I drew the symbols, then went over to explain it in person that night. We stood in front of his desk and pulled up the file I'd sent: the Schrodinger equation. I deciphered it: psi, phi, superscripted squares. Explained the superposition of probabilities. He furrowed his brow, following my line of reasoning. He didn't yet know that I often calculated probabilities in my head, estimating the chances he'd leave his wife for me.

He looked at the monitor and stood close behind me, his groin just below my hips. I shifted a little, but he didn't move. I turned around, moved away, pointed from a different angle.

His eyes moved from the screen and bored through me. He took my elbows. I looked up at him. He leaned in.

When his head was a foot from mine, I ducked and said very quietly, "Stop. This is wrong. You're married."

He straightened up, still cupping my elbows with his hands. "I'm in love with you . . . and I'm married," he said.

I stood, eyes wide. My mouth silently opened and shut. No grown man had ever before admitted to being in love with me. I felt at once giddy and flattered and frightened of getting in trouble.

He let go of my elbows, looked down. "Come on," he said quietly, "I'll walk you home."

How could he say this, spin me around, and then send me away, like a puppy he'd grown tired of? It seemed like only a few days since I had stopped by with an empty thermos. In reality, it had been six weeks; the civilian attraction timeline had compressed. At home (and pre-Tinder), this dance could have taken six months. As we crossed the gravel path toward Tent City, my frustration surged. I wondered what I could say to bring back his attention.

I said, "Where the fuck do you get off? You're married!"

They weren't exactly the right words.

"I'm sorry, but . . . you keep coming back," he said. "Should I never speak to you again?"

Never again? I thought. It wasn't a conversation I could leave hanging. So we bypassed my tent, headed to the tea garden, and faced off in chairs at our usual tree. I wanted him to explain more, to say what he was thinking and feeling and planning. To lay this out for me, so I could have some idea of how to respond. Everything felt uncertain, but I wanted certainty. More than anything, I wanted him to tell me over and over how great I was.

"What the hell am I supposed to do now?" I said.

He looked down, searched for words, finally put on a paternal smile. "You're something special," he said, "and don't ever let anyone tell you different."

"Thanks," I said. But I wanted more. A guarantee. Something that would confirm his mind orbited me, that he would stay with me, would choose to be with only me.

Instead he said, "Even if nothing ever comes of this, I'm just glad to know you."

I nodded, adrenaline roiling. "Uh-huh. Me too."

It was late. Though there was everything more to say, neither of us spoke. Truth be told, I was also nervous. If our colleagues found out, the consequences could prove far worse than the vulnerability of a leaked middle-school crush; we could face disciplinary action. And Jack and I both had to be awake again in a matter of hours—another blazing sunrise and Groundhog Day slog.

As he walked me back to my tent, we remained silent. I wondered if we'd see each other again soon, or if our conversation had put a stop to everything. I parted the tent flap.

"As a friend," I said, "I love you, too."

• • •

It seemed that all of us in Comm Company felt tormented in different ways. One afternoon toward the end of June, I climbed a metal ladder and heaved open the heavy green door to the switchboard van. Despite decades of use, it still smelled like lead paint. Inside, a Spanish-soap DVD played on the old TV the Marines had snuck into the embark shipment. Thin Corporal Allenton crunched through a bag of Doritos, headphones on, air-conditioner shirring her loose T-shirt. Nothing seemed to put any meat on her. The staff sergeant had tried giving her protein shakes, PowerBars, anything to get her weight up. "Hey, ma'am," she said, slipping off an oversized earphone.

"How's it going?" I asked.

"Comm's good," she said, "but Corporal Kim's out back. He's having a rough time."

Corporal Kim was one of our most stable Marines. The quiet son of Korean immigrants, he was a hardworking, uncomplaining kid who'd enlisted out of high school in his native San Francisco. So far he'd been zero trouble. I left Allenton to her show, shut the airtight door, and crept around the foot-wide deck made from metal strips. Kim sat on an MRE box, a cigarette between his shaking fingers. I pulled up a crate. We were hidden on a platform between two switchboard vans, above the generators, where no one could see or hear. It was a good place to cry.

A Red Cross message had come for Kim earlier that day; his mom had had a stroke. Through tears, he told me she was all right, hospitalized but recovering.

I rummaged in my pocket for the chow-hall napkins I usually stashed, but all I touched was a Ziploc bag of crushed tampons. Kim wiped his nose on his cammie blouse, cradling his M16 with wiry forearms.

There was more. He'd found out his ex-girlfriend was sleeping with his best friend back home. "I'm pissed at him, but I forgive her," he said, and shuddered a sob. "I just want her back. I can't deal with this."

Fuck. I couldn't deal with this, either.

"I know it hurts," I said, bewildered, hoping my presence helped a little. I couldn't figure out my own love life; I was in no position to counsel my Marines on theirs. Kim looked at me, red-faced. He wrung his boonie cover and wiped his nose again.

"We need you out here," I stammered, "and you're doing a damn fine job." Kim pulled cable without complaint, kept his weapon clean, played video games with the other Californians in Wire Platoon's tent.

He said that before the war, gangsters had carjacked his girlfriend in Oakland. Now that he was deployed, he couldn't protect her. And he still wanted to, even though she was now with his best friend. Nor could he help his sick mother. "There's just so much pressure," he said. "It's getting to me."

I started to worry. I remembered the Father's Day suicide of that nineteen-year-old PFC, the one tormented by an ass-chewing after he forgot to shave.

"I'm not worried about your girlfriend," I said, "I'm worried about you. I'm not her lieutenant, I'm yours." I owed it to Corporal Kim to help him with his problems, to have a wise answer ready.

He looked at me skeptically and sniffled. Tears started to dry into tracks.

"It'll be all right," I promised. "Your place is here. We need you here. You're doing a great job." Cliché roulette.

Kim sat, polite and quiet. I clapped him on the shoulder, told him again that we needed him here. That he was going to be all right. That he should hang out with the platoon and talk with the sergeants about this. *Or the staff sergeant*, I thought to myself. *Or the gunny. Or anyone more qualified than me.*

He ran a tanned hand through his buzz cut before mashing his cover back on. "Thanks, ma'am," he mumbled as we clambered down the ladder. I spied the gunny and motioned him over, hoping I'd done no harm. In this, I wasn't alone; rare is the lieutenant whose twenty-odd years of life experience spans enough to support wise, impromptu relationship counseling.

The thing I *was* potentially qualified to do, I wanted no part of. Maybe, as I headed into the SYSCON, I could have counseled the stocky Staff Sergeant Hermano on proper phone-fighting etiquette with his soon-to-be ex-wife.

Standing watch with him meant turning up the volume on my earbuds and trying not to eavesdrop. Although I didn't speak Spanish, it was difficult to ignore. A vein stood out on his bald scalp as he fumed over custody arrangements and child support, until all I heard was "TAMBIEN! TAMBIEN!" roared across the room. I began to understand the corollaries to my parents' frustrations, the distant halves of the muffled phone-shouts, the deepening ruts of hatred as they replayed the same arguments year after year. Sweat shone on Hermano's forehead as he seethed. I wasn't precisely sure of the source of his anger. But his wife might have taken issue with his impregnating a female corporal in his platoon.

Gunny Duncan, the multichannel radio platoon commander, remained philosophical about situations like these. His current wife was his third; he loved her and his two teenage stepkids. But he'd walked a rough road before. "Just because you had a failed marriage," he said, "doesn't make you a failure."

I mulled this over, sipping coffee after the SYSCON had quieted. So much of my own story rested on blaming my parents—I insisted they'd destroyed my childhood. I decided that Gunny Duncan might be right for himself, maybe even for Hermano. I'd spent months silently witnessing my Marines' vulnerabilities. But when it came to my folks, I figured the good gunny had to be wrong.

And as for myself and my own situation with Jack, I thought, *I could die anytime. Then it won't matter whether or not I've lived by the rules.*

For grounding and solace one morning, I called the apartment where three college friends lived together, back in Cambridge. They'd been my intellectual link to the civilian world ever since I'd been the sole ROTC-uniformed freshman in our dorm.

They scrambled to the phone once they realized it was me. One girl, Ellen, strummed a song I'd written on guitar; I almost cried at the familiar chords. The words were a silly parody about Jake, my old lab partner, and his tendency to do everything at the last minute. On the phone, Jake said he'd gotten into Oxford for grad school. He would move to England that December for a doctoral program in computational bioinformatics. I offered congratulations and said I was happy for him. Inside I crumbled with envy.

When I hung up, I felt even emptier than when I'd dialed. My friends were all moving on, racking up degrees, practicing instruments, continuing romances. And where was I? Sitting at a plywood desk in the desert, shuffling through emails and awaiting the next mortar attack. It didn't seem as valuable.

Senior year in college, the Harvard-trained endodontist who'd removed my wisdom teeth had called my Marine Corps commission "a waste of a degree." He had seemed rude at the time, but he was the one looming over me with a foot-long needle, so I thought it best not to provoke him. Now it looked like he was right, like my friends and I would all have gone our separate ways by the time I was released from the military. Their voices still rang in my ears. I wouldn't be back in Boston anytime soon. As my watch shift ticked along, I doubted my contributions to the war—or the world. What the hell was I doing in a concrete hut in Iraq, surrounded by men with disintegrating marriages?

• • •

On a slow evening a few weeks after phoning my friends, I opened a former labmate's care package to find *Cool as Ice*—Vanilla Ice's first and only movie. The staff NCOs hooted at the cheesy DVD cover, then encouraged Marla and me to take a break from the SYSCON to watch it with Major Davis. *Officer time*, they said. *Get out of our hair*, they meant.

Armed with Twizzlers, Marla and I tromped up to the Major's palatial wooden hut and projected the movie on a wall that usually displayed PowerPoints and network diagrams. We laughed at Vanilla Ice and reminisced about Hypercolor shirts and eight-ball jackets; though Marla had grown up all over the world, and the major had been in college in the early '90s, the garish fads were hard to forget. It was the best non-Jack evening I'd had in a while, but even so, its end left me staring at my boots. When Marla left for her watch shift, I stayed a few minutes longer on the plywood bench. Major Davis sensed my mind was elsewhere.

"T, what's up? You're quiet."

"Sir . . ." I swallowed hard. "I'm kinda bummed. My old lab partner got into Oxford for grad school. And I'm here. I mean, what'm I doing out here?"

He leaned in, put his forearms on his knees. "I knew this

was coming sooner or later," he said. "Listen. Not everyone can do your job. Your Marines need you. You're doing valuable work here."

"I am?" I said, slouched and skeptical. *Even though you chewed my ass about the fiber yesterday? Even though all I can do is ride along in a dusty Humvee every week, checking the lines, rattling toward oblivion? Even though I trot behind you and my staff NCOs, just trying to keep up, screwing up more days than not?*

My Marines didn't seem to need me. My staff NCOs knew much more than I did. I was probably just in the way.

But the major went on: "You're on the world stage. This is a once-in-a-lifetime opportunity. Your friends back home will never get the chance to lead Marines in a combat zone."

"Yeah, I know," I said, unconvinced.

"You're a damn good Marine officer, T," he said.

I looked up. *Am I?*

"This may come easy to you, but it doesn't come easy to everybody. In two years, I hope you'll stay in, but you're only young once. Follow your dreams. Grad school will be there when you get back."

The major thought I was good? I'd been so down on myself, I hadn't thought he might actually praise me. I stifled a smile, felt a zing of pride. "Thanks, sir," I squeaked, and gathered my cover and CamelBak.

As I walked down his short flight of wood steps, I thought maybe my fellow troops did find me valuable. I certainly needed them in order to feel any sense of purpose. And as much as I doubted myself, maybe something I said to Corporal Kim— maybe—had helped him feel more positive, just as the major had helped me. An uneasy guilt hit the back of my throat as I remembered Jack's hug.

What it would take me years to learn is that it didn't matter what job I'd taken after college graduation. I would learn what I was meant to about love and friendship—and a leader's integrity—no matter whether I spent my days in a prestigious physics program, an entry-level office job, or a war. Mortars and convoys made for an unusual backdrop, sure. But the same types of scenarios, the same moral choices, and similar lessons would have presented themselves, regardless of where I landed.

NINE

Beatings Will Continue until Morale Improves

Nights, Jack and I paired up to teach martial arts. Our class numbered about fifty Marines, nearly all from Comm Company, with a few from Mortuary Affairs. Word had gotten out that passing our courses helped troops get promoted, and that they could work off stress by wrestling their buddies. My mostly good-hearted troops had brains enough to program crypto, splice cable, repair switchboards and laptops, and run videoconferences. While I cared about their technical skills, I also had to ensure they weren't raping anyone or dealing drugs or siphoning internet porn—I wanted them too exhausted and bruised to even consider any of that. So my purpose was twofold: to ensure they could protect themselves and to tire them out so much that they wouldn't get into trouble. Sergeant Mullins and Lance Corporal Sanchez usually helped teach, even if just hours prior they'd been cleaning up bodies.

We started class at 2100, when the temperature dipped below ninety. Night descended swiftly after the sherbet sunset, so we borrowed a floodlight from the Mortuary Affairs platoon. Lance Corporal Kowalczek—a six-foot-six, deuce-and-a-half Marine who had emigrated from Poland in elementary school—dragged it the hundred yards to our rock-strewn sandpit. Illuminated in neat rows of ten, the troops traded insults and whacked each other's limbs for "body hardening." Jack stood in the back and stretched his shoulders.

I had plotted out drills in my notebook: five stations in the corners and center of a 50-by-50-foot sandpit. Marines practiced hip throws in the center and upper-body strikes, knee strikes, wrestling, and sit-ups in the corners. We timed them at two minutes per station. In between, they bear-crawled, forward-rolled, crab-walked, and fireman's-carried each other.

Among the instructors, innuendo ran rampant. To demonstrate a weapon of opportunity, Sergeant Mullins held a length of pipe wrapped in electrical tape and winked as he told sparring partners to grab his "big rod." Sanchez gossiped about accidentally interrupting Marla peeing in the Porta-John: "What's the difference between her and a kitten? One's cute and furry, and the other one's a cat!" I smirked, said nothing to Sanchez, and told Mullins, "only if it's stiff." Rolling with dirty jokes signaled power and inclusion.

The ways I'd devised to surprise my students also lent me an air of mischief. During a drill involving Marines lying supine, elbowing furiously at their partners holding pads atop them, I jumped on the pad-holders' backs to add pressure. On the street, if they did not know me, these men could have swatted me away. But here in the pit, they laughed with me, and I with them. As in middle-school playground football, I felt like one of them, even when thrown or pinned. I wasn't a girl or guy or anyone's sidekick; I was a Marine. When the drills ended, we were sweaty and sandy, breathing heavily.

I also taught hip throws. I wedged my right hip under Mullins's, grabbing his right wrist with my left hand. I spun my left foot behind me, tracing out a little "c." As I swiveled, he flipped down on the sand—a big arc through the air.

Little arc, big arc, I thought. Small choices led to big ones. Seemingly insignificant details like foot placement became the foundation on which you staked the rest of your fight. Whatever little steps I'd taken, there was always another move, another bout. Only the circumstances—those with whom I wrestled—

would change. Meanwhile, Jack stood on the outskirts of the circle, preparing to practice knife fighting.

Some Marines borrowed rounded rubber blades from our meager official supply. Others brought sheathed bayonets, while a few had pocketed plastic knives from the chow hall. To supplement, I grabbed a few dozen chemlights—six-inch glow sticks popular with suburban trick-or-treaters—from Radio Platoon. The chemlights' plastic innards cracked, activating the glow. With a few whistle blasts, I signaled slashes, thrusts, and parries. My Marines slashed their chemlights on cue. Training looked from a distance like a very sandy rave.

Soon an angry man in a flight suit cut through the crowd. His collar bore a gold leaf, and he was pissed. "Who's in charge here?" the major demanded. He cocked an appraising eye at Jack.

Jack sounded off tartly, "Lieutenant Fazio's in charge!" and snuck me a grin, his eyebrows high, as if he was faking helpfulness.

"Thanks, asshole," I muttered.

The major stalked up to me. My forehead came level with the insignia pinned to his flight suit. He was breathing hard; his uniform hid a paunchy belly. He raised an index finger at our floodlight. "Turn that damn light in the opposite direction!" he screamed. "You're blinding the pilots!"

In our glee at breaking the monotony, we hadn't even thought of the floodlight's position.

"Sir, we—we didn't know. I'm sorry, sir," I spluttered.

"*Think* next time you turn one of those goddamn things on," he spat. I glanced back at Kowalczek, who reversed the light's aim.

I snapped to attention as the major stalked off. The Marines kicked their boot-toes in the sand. The chemlights lay piled in a corner of the sandpit, some still glowing weakly. Fighting my embarrassment, I formed them up for the next exercise. "I thought you handled that well," Jack might have said in a soothing tone. It's the kind of thing he would have said to calm me, to make me forgive him for throwing me under the bus. At least

I had gotten yelled at for something fixable, not something as shameful as being discovered *in flagrante*. Even as I paired up to be fireman's-carried or coached a Marine to pivot his heel and throw his weight behind a punch, I sensed where Jack stood. His Marines said nothing when I disappeared behind his door after martial arts, under the guise of either TV-watching decompression or planning our next class. Visiting openly seemed to preserve my reputation, or maybe I was convincingly androgynous and puckish enough to not be suspected. Only when we practiced wrestling on his fake-linoleum floor did I consciously let down my guard. He taught me a choking move, the soft crook of his elbow brushing my lips as he wound his arm around me. Mimicking him, I wrapped my right bicep beside his neck and compressed his carotid artery with my forearm, driving him to the verge of unconsciousness. He swam up out of my hold, at once gentle and powerful, saying he would never hurt me.

TEN

Everything Goes to Shit

Deployment Day plus Five Months

July was the month that everything went to shit. Within the first few days, our main telephone switchboard died, its cards frying in 131-degree heat. Nothing would resurrect it, though my technician played whack-a-mole with multimeter and soldering iron during two all-nighters. The death of a long-overused air conditioner dealt the switchboard a fatal blow. Then the generators powering the entire communications site succumbed to sand and grit. We cursed the equipment for several days. Another unit would loan us an air conditioner, but it was too big for even Kowalczek to heft on his own.

So, at 0200 one morning, knowing he'd still be awake, I called Jack to ask for a favor.

"Can you get me a forklift?" I asked, trying to sound nonchalant.

"Of course," he said. "I'm your hero."

Within hours, he'd cut a deal with some logisticians. A small forklift ambled toward our compound, its prongs bearing a six-foot-tall air conditioner just for us.

"I owe you one," I told Jack on the phone. "I owe you, like, a million."

"Don't worry," he said. "I'll come collect."

• • •

July also marked the transition of sovereignty to the Iraqis. Any political event, even fifty miles away in Baghdad, fired up the insurgents more than usual. One quiet morning I was in front of my laptop on SYSCON watch. Staff Sergeant Hermano slouched behind the watch chief's desk, earbuds cranking music. Lance Corporal Roberts had just entered to report the status of the radio nets and nose around our snack stash. I was contemplating a second cup of coffee when the mortar hit.

We felt the blast before we heard it. It shook the cement SYSCON hut.

I stood at my desk, not wanting to look afraid by getting under it.

Another mortar hit. Hermano dove under his desk. Roberts hunkered under the sturdy table where we kept the logbooks.

I ducked under my plywood desk and shimmied into my flak jacket, then picked up my Kevlar helmet and cradled it awkwardly.

Roberts had left his own helmet back in the radio tent.

It would be selfish of me to put this on, I thought. *I should plonk it on Roberts's head.*

But I didn't. Instead I placed it on the floor near him, silent, feeling stupid. He didn't pick it up, just stared at me as if I were an idiot.

We waited a minute, not speaking. No more mortars fell.

When I peeked my head over the desk, the screen showed a downed fiber optic connection to group headquarters. *Fuck.* I started making phone calls, testing the lines.

Lance Corporal Roberts hung out in the SYSCON, bareheaded, till we got the all-clear from battalion.

Though in later years I would have nightmares of dodging mortars, it would be hours that day before I learned just how lucky we'd been. In the late afternoon I went to the blast site, only fifty yards away. It had turned a tent into Swiss cheese. I parted the flap. Sunlight streamed through jagged holes. Shredded canvas fluttered in the breeze. I shuddered, thinking what the scene would have been if the tent had been occupied.

Our fiber, which had been zip-tied along some sand-filled Hesco barriers, was shredded. Shrapnel had splayed open the cable's plastic casing. I had never liked the insurgents, but now I was righteously pissed.

Later, as I finished making reports—no casualties, fiber lines down—Staff Sergeant Hermano jerked his chin doorward. "You have a visitor, ma'am."

Nathan, my college boyfriend, banged through the SYSCON's metal door. He looped an arm over my shoulder, a chaste hug. The sun had browned his freckled arms and face. I'd forgotten how tall he was. We'd been broken up for three years, and I hadn't seen him since Quantico. Now ROTC felt like kid stuff. I was suddenly conscious of my dirty uniform.

"Sorry, they lost my laundry a week ago," I said, as our hug ended.

He sniffed his own blouse. "I'm wearing my one clean set of cammies."

As an infantry platoon commander, Nathan had been patrolling the areas outside Abu Ghraib. As we found out on the chow hall's TV—but nowhere else—what was going on *inside* the prison at that point proved far more of a problem. He glanced out the window, keeping tabs on his radio operator. The kid smoked a cigarette outside the SYSCON, still humping the PRC-119F radio, its antenna taped down. The receiver emitted a ghost of static every few seconds. They were heading to Ramadi, about twenty-five miles west of us. The Marines there were taking heavy casualties.

"How you doin'?" I asked, cocking my head to catch Nathan's eye.

He shrugged. "Eh, you know."

"This is weird, but I'm glad you're not dead."

He barked a hoarse laugh. "Yeah, I'm glad you're not dead, either."

Random encounters like this proved surprisingly common while deployed: classmates, spouses, siblings, even parents and children ran into each other. We snapped a picture for our old college buddies, one more hug, and he was on his way.

• • •

On our next movie night, Jack, Mullins, a couple of sergeants, and I crammed into Jack's room to watch *South Park*. Mullins handed us ropes of Nerds candy, care-package goodies from his wife. We chewed and laughed, riding sugar highs, hearing dropped Nerds bounce out of reach. Midway through the movie, the phone rang at the Mortuary Affairs watch desk. We held our breath. A Marine appeared in the doorway; a surgical patient had died of wounds. Jack, in scrubs, leapt to his sneakered feet, grinding spilled Nerds into fake linoleum. He jabbed "pause" on the movie, and he and Mullins and their Marines headed out the door. I walked back to my tent and chanted a decade of my rosary to hasten sleep. I still hadn't gotten used to the long empty stretches punctuated by frantic activity— activity from which I was shut out.

Jack told me about it the next day, though. The chaplain, after administering last rites, had raided his fridge for Coke Light. Ducking into the room, he was startled by Jack's laptop screen, still paused to the scene where a cartoon Satan was in bed with a dick-obsessed Saddam Hussein.

• • •

A few mornings after, I scrolled through the SIPRnet on SYSCON watch: four KIAs near Fallujah, and Mortuary Affairs had already left the wire to recover the burned-out bodies. Jack was on a convoy. A little knowledge was a dangerous thing; I always felt anxious when he left the wire. Knowing I couldn't communicate with him directly, I tried turning to someone closer to my age and farther from the fight: my most recent ex, Ben, back in Quantico, who'd written me with tales of his hamster.

But this tactic backfired. Instead of a distractingly pleasant conversation, it turned out Ben wanted answers to questions like, "Are you sticking around in the Marine Corps?" (*Hell no!*) and, "What are my chances with you?" (*Pretty slim.*) I spent the morning in frustration behind the plywood SYSCON desk.

Early that afternoon, Clive walked in. He complained, as usual, that my platoon wasn't getting the fiber underground fast enough. I leaned forward, elbows on my knees, hands wringing the brim of my cover. Sweat pooled on my back. As I answered his questions, my voice choked, first imperceptibly, then harder, until I couldn't hold back ragged breaths. Clive noticed that whatever was wrong didn't involve data cables. He brayed through his mustache: "What the fuck's goin' on, T? C'mon, what the fuck's goin' on?"

What's going on, I thought, *is that the guy I love might die any minute on a convoy.*

I couldn't tell Clive—he and the major would string me up the flagpole, and whatever respect the rest of the battalion had for me would evaporate. My Marines would laugh, trade knowing glances, and treat me like they treated Marla.

I distracted Clive with tales of Ben, how he wanted to know if he had a future with me.

"Tell you what, T, you got plenty of time; what're you, twenny-three?" Clive said. "You gotta do what's best for you. If this guy doesn't work out, I bet there'll be all sortsa young beach dudes after you. C'mon, it's Southern California." He continued with well-intentioned platitudes to which I paid no attention. I tuned back in to hear, "You're way too stressed out, T. We gotta get some beer into you."

I'd heard scuttlebutt about the wife he called Momma sending him a care package of Budweiser, maybe something stronger, in Listerine bottles.

"Nah, that's okay," I said.

I wasn't about to get up in Clive's business about his drinking. Convoys, mortars, and rockets made everyday actions a dice roll, and plenty of folks made choices that fell short of legality. For me, nights with Jack felt like my only source of true human connection, and I cared about his safety far more than my own. A combat zone was the worst—and yet most intense and seductive—place in the world for Clive to sneak a few beers, or for me to fall in love.

That afternoon I copied a passage from *Gates of Fire*, a novel about the battle of Thermopylae, into my notebook. The Greek soldiers' equivalent of dog tags—their tickets—were torn into civilian and warrior halves as they went into battle:

> When a man . . . steps off from the line of departure . . . He marches into battle bearing only . . . that half which knows slaughter and butchery and turns the blind eye to quarter.

It felt like that for me, too. When Jack's convoy safely returned, I figured *to hell with civilized relationships*.

• • •

Stress mounted on Camp Taqaddum as convoys pulsed and mortars threatened, and at the end of July, I found myself in Jack's room on the night of his birthday. After a movie, he whispered he loved me by the blue electron glow of his laptop screen. We stood and stretched, high on burnt popcorn and Coke Light. His muscled forearms slunk around my waist.

For once, when he leaned down, I looked up. I didn't flinch. My eyes shut as he moved closer, until all I felt were his smooth lips and cool tongue. Much more tongue than I was used to, frankly. He hadn't shaved since morning; dark stubble grazed my cheek.

When we were done making out, he said, "You're a good kisser," and chuckled.

"Why are you laughing?" I said.

"I'm just glad I didn't get hit for kissing you," he said.

When I fell asleep, a curtain fell with me. It was a flat blade of secrecy, like a shovel to the skull. I rustled from my cot the next morning, groggy, shrugging off guilt. By the time I trotted to the SYSCON with my to-go plate of eggs and bread, I'd pushed the kiss from my mind. If I didn't think about it—and if I never let anyone find out—I could let myself return.

ELEVEN

Laying Cable

Deployment Day plus Six Months

I sat in an empty SYSCON on the morning of my twenty-fourth birthday, while my exhausted Marines dug trenches and laid fiber on what was supposed to have been their day off. I removed my pistol from my holster. It shone dully, little bits of the blacking scraped off. I wiped its barrel with the end of my T-shirt. *This should be cleaner*, I thought.

• • •

In early August, we had a month and a half left in the deployment. The advance party of replacements would arrive in three weeks. It seemed like forever. Though we still could get mortared any minute, midmonth would mark was the longest Jack had gone without an angel: nineteen days. His room remained my sanctuary.

The rules about walking solo had slackened. After midnight, I simply chambered a round in my pistol and went where I wanted. I let Jack kiss me by his room's slop sink, where he'd vomited from food poisoning and boiled tea water for grieving Iraqi families. When I was there, he said, none of that mattered. He felt safe. I did, too.

He'd ditched the mosquito-net canopy from his "princess bed." He slid his hands under my arms, lifted me and threw me onto it. My boots hit his shins. He didn't wince, only moved his pistol to a plywood shelf.

He lay back in his scrubs. I was T-shirted, trousered, and booted. By the light of his desk lamp, we held each other. My glasses fogged when I drowsed on his chest. Tight muscles relaxed.

We turned to our sides, facing each other. His fingers drummed lightly on my hip.

"When we get home," he said, "I just want to cuddle you. Just like this, in a fluffy white bed, until we're too hungry to stay any longer."

"Mm-hmm," I murmured.

"If you could be anywhere, where would you be?" he asked. By circling the small of my back with his fingertip, he pushed a boundary, but technically we were keeping ourselves in line.

Though I'd wanted to go home for months, Iraq now felt more real than home. And Jack felt more real than anyone I'd been with before. While we clasped each other, we staved off the world. "I don't want to be anywhere except right here with you," I said.

His desk phone rang, a short repeating trill. This meant that it was coming from off our base, from a surgical hospital or operations center elsewhere in Iraq. Hell, it could even be from the States, though it would have to be from a military base—it was impossible for civilian phones to call us back.

Jack answered, "Mortuary Affairs."

I sat up.

"Yeah. Okay. We'll be here," he said.

He replaced the slim black handset, turned and lifted me to stand.

"Four dead kids."

Outside our base near the Euphrates, a convoy had been traveling double the 20-mph speed limit, because what idiot stuck around when you were halfway between Fallujah and Baghdad? A Humvee had hit a pothole and flipped into the river.

Water rose swiftly, trapping the Marines inside. They couldn't open the doors. The staff NCOs roped and winched the vehicle; still the hitches slipped, and the doors were gunked shut. Nothing worked. Panicked young faces soon froze under wet glass. Four dead kids.

I did not yet know that the circumstances closely matched those of a convoy led by another lieutenant from my graduation year. With liquid brown eyes and a quick smile, he'd been raised among Long Island women by a beautician mom. On all-too-brief weekends that punctuated our training in Quantico woods, I'd watched him speak easily to the ladies, always sweetly chivalrous, with the long-lashed gaze that had won him his young wife.

Now he'd see those kids in his dreams. I'd imagine the vision of four dead kids with him for years, their faces white and pleading through murky windows. Colonels and generals would question him harshly, "Why where you going so goddamned fast, son?" *Because we didn't want to get shot at*, everyone knew. But it didn't matter. In the hearings that would follow, the Marine Corps would imply that the accident had been his fault.

When the phone rang, I had not yet heard this. All I knew was that I had to go back to my tent, the rapid parting from Jack that happened more nights than not. He handed me my CamelBak. I left through his secret door that opened directly to the outside, so his Marines couldn't see me exit. Later I would find out they thought the door's squeak behind me signaled ghosts. Working in Mortuary Affairs bred superstition.

On the walk back to my tent, I stumbled over cables. The TA-1042 field telephone handset just needed a bit of wire to connect it, the kind one might buy at a hardware store. At the Basic School, that unlucky convoy commander and I had knelt in muddy fields and learned to wire the terminals to a switchboard. We had gripped wire strippers, clenched gently, and shucked sleeves of plastic insulation, exposing four copper lines and three sharp steel cables. We'd separated the ductile strands, bending the copper away, rolling it between our fingertips and wrapping it around the steel to improve the wires' conductivity—the better to bear more bad news.

When I slipped through my tent flap that night, the space was quiet, save for a humming air conditioner. As I fell asleep, I remembered reports unsent, papers unsigned, letters and emails unwritten. I felt too tired to pull my notebook from my cargo pocket and scribble reminders for anyone, living or dead.

• • •

A few nights later, when there were no casualties, Jack and I stared at each other in his room, drinking near-beer. His daily mantra hadn't wavered: "I'm just trying to get through today." He said I was saving his life.

I was tired but didn't want to go yet. "What's gonna happen when we get back to Pendleton?" I asked.

He sighed. "This is not a math problem, T. Six and four don't always make ten. When are you going to stop trying to analyze everything?"

"I don't know," I said, and dropped my forehead into my palms.

"Being on this deployment with you is amazing," he said. "And I wouldn't trade it for anything."

Sitting on my cot that night, I weighed options and made mental flowcharts, trying to wring an answer from the brain that had once made me proud. I thought of ifs, ands, truth unions, Venn diagrams. I thought if I could just find a thread of logic through all of this, if I could figure out the "right answer," I could simultaneously be with Jack and have the permanent love and acceptance of my fellow Marines.

Ever the scientist, I tried to gather data and submit my thoughts for peer review. In my previous life, there had been classmates to ask about problem sets, solutions to compare and re-write before sliding brittle sheets of Guinness-stained equations into the grader's locked box. Maybe I still knew people with the answers.

Maddie, a friend from both high school and college, knew What To Do About Guys. I pictured her curly hair, her fashionable wrap dresses, her flirtatious confidence. She'd never judged me through the years for my hookups or unrequited crushes. And she had good reason to keep tabs on me; she'd be picking me up at Camp Pendleton when I returned. Complete with brackets, she wrote,

[disapproving nod] You kissed him?! I know you know better . . . please don't do anything illegal—and don't tempt yourself . . . unfortunately, it's too late for me to send you a vibrator.

I'd also written Ellen, the guitar-playing college friend who had different advice:

You have to take these chances when they appear to you, because you have to embrace life and love while you can. It's all bound to be bittersweet; LIFE is bittersweet. Timing is ever a heinous bitch; that's the kicker, of course: the thought that maybe things could work out if not for the circumstance. But. Never mind that. We have to be open to love and to loss, or else we truly lose.

I tucked Maddie's letter inside Ellen's letter and carried both in my cargo pocket. I pulled them out to read when I was alone. The stationery dampened with sweat, dried, got damp again. I was mired in conflicting advice. This called for reinforcements.

I thought of my high school band director, Ms. Hopper. Junior year, for history-class projects on "the biography of a woman hero," most kids picked their moms or famous historical figures. I'd picked her. Though I could never bring myself to call her by her first name, we'd stayed in touch; I'd last emailed her before deploying.

I found the small office by the SYSCON finally quiet enough for a private phone call. I dialed the glowing touch-tone buttons, cupped a palm round the slimline receiver. And on an oak-lined street in suburban New York, she picked up her landline.

"Teresa! What a surprise! Aren't you in—"

"Iraq. Yeah. Actually I have a quick question for you."

I also knew a secret of hers, loosed by an upperclassman crush in backstage whispers—her husband was much older than she was. When they'd met, he had been married, with children.

I said, "I heard you were nineteen when you met your husband, and that he's a lot older than you are."

"Twenty-two years older," she said cautiously.

"And I heard, um—I heard when you met him he was still married."

"That's correct," she said, clipped and far away. She didn't know I knew this. But I plowed on.

"And his kids were still little."

"Things happened." I could hear her lips tighten. I'd never asked her anything personal, ever.

I shook as I said, "There's this guy . . ." and my story spilled out.

No one was in the concrete office, but I ducked my head behind my laptop screen. The first sergeant entered, a blast of hot air from the dented metal door. I murmured low uh-huhs and choked back tears. He saw I was on a personal phone call and politely backed away. The door hinges groaned.

Ms. Hopper softened her tone. "Try to keep a distance. Don't make any rash decisions over there. Don't make ANY decisions. This will sort itself out when you come home."

"Really?"

"The thing is, you have a choice between the easy route and the complicated route."

"What's the easy route?"

"Don't see him. Forget it."

I couldn't do that.

"If it's real, it'll last," she said. "But only you know whether this is real."

The next day, she emailed me:

Life is complicated, no question about it. I am sure that you
will do the right thing—for you and all concerned. Finding
the right thing is the difficulty and ultimately only you will
know what it is. Everyone else, and I mean everyone, is on
the outside looking in. Good luck.

I didn't know what the right thing was. I only knew that
in the moments I stole with Jack, I delighted in a feminine
power I'd never before known, and felt safe and cared for in a
place of destruction and death. Then, in the bleak hours after
leaving his room, my hold on his attention seemed a shallow
mirage—one his marriage would soon supersede. I spiraled
into self-flagellation, counting among my faults a lack of officer's integrity, compounded by untoward, messy desire. Even
as I googled the UCMJ to find whether a kiss was forgivable, I
knew moral responsibility landed squarely on my shoulders.
This is how we were trained to be, as Marine officers—to hold
ourselves personally accountable in a violent, chaotic environment. So, day by day, I strove to have it both ways: maintaining
a lieutenant's outward diligence while drinking in Jack's attention. I thought I could pull it off, if I tried hard enough. It all
seemed to rest on my shoulders.

All this pressure needed a release valve. So, every few nights
I still walked to Jack's bunker, tiptoeing out the back door as its
sliver of yellow light disappeared.

• • •

In mid-August, as my birthday approached, the schedule for the
sixteen Marines in my wire platoon revolved around digging and
chow. While I stood watch behind a desk in an air-conditioned
SYSCON, they toiled in the heat. After loading a jackhammer
and Ditch Witch into a Humvee at dawn, they drove out to dig
knee-deep trenches along the base's silent, sun-baked perimeter. They returned for lunch, drenched in sweat, and drove
back down the lonely road in the late afternoon. At dusk they

returned caked in sand, with rings of salt on their boonie covers. My Marines all sported deep farmer tans and more muscle than in the months before; a few had grown mustaches. They'd been laying cable for five of our seven months in country. But the farthest-out units still weren't getting wired up fast enough, and Major Davis chewed my ass about inadequately protected fiber. I felt inadequate, too; by working long hours, with martial arts and mortuary affairs the only breaks, I'd driven myself to the edge of burnout.

"Have you been to this intersection, T?" the major asked one morning, after finding more fiber exposed to heavy vehicle traffic. Whenever I thought things were quiet, it just meant that another strand of cable was fraying that I didn't yet know about. Why was there even an inch of unprotected cable visible? Why wasn't the entire base wired in yet?

At 0600 on the day before my birthday, I made a circuit of tent city, running first to the airfield entryway, then to the dirt road that led out past the buried airplanes. I could see the dark rut across the road that meant we had laid cables there, but only a few sandbags and ripped cardboard sheets protected them. My Marines might as well have laid Kleenex. Heavy vehicles could cut through in a heartbeat. Worse, our fiber cleaver—the device that let us clip the cable cleanly in order to fuse it back together—was broken. We had to borrow one from another unit, which delayed repair time. I hated being the bad cop.

It was only 0630 by the time I finished my run-through of the fiber line, but I went directly to Staff Sergeant Garcia's tent and slipped through the flap, into the dark interior. Most of the staff NCOs were out cold; I could make out sleeping-bagged humps a few cots over. Garcia had the cot closest to the door. I hesitated, not wanting to invade their space. Then I put a hand on Garcia's T-shirted shoulder and shook him awake. He looked stunned; I must have seemed like a little green-clad desert elf.

"Ma'am?" he said, wincing. His back must have knotted and

seized again. I wondered if he needed more of those muscle relaxers the docs had prescribed.

"The fiber by the flight line's unprotected. I need the Marines to get on it."

"We'll get on it, ma'am," he said, then shifted in his cot. He did not make a move to get up.

I must have pressed harder, saying, "soon" or "this morning" or perhaps even "now." I didn't think to concoct a deadline, though I would later berate myself for not doing so, for falling short of righteous anger, for being so conflict-averse. But I knew someone would be pissed at me no matter how I handled this. If everyone knew what the end outcome needed to be—that we needed the cable buried—why did I have to be in the middle and "lead"?

• • •

These frustrations consumed me as I ruminated on the following morning, my birthday, with my weapon in my lap. The last time I'd cleaned it, I'd wiped down the bullets, too, slicing my cuticles as I filed them into the magazine.

I reached for the magazine now, those ten bullets inside. Unsnapped the green nylon pouch. It slid out smoothly.

I slipped the magazine into my weapon, helped along by a light coat of lubricant. The release button jiggled and clicked into place.

I leaned in, with my elbows on my knees, pretending to handle my weapon idly under the desk. But Marines don't handle weapons idly.

I slid off the safety. A two-millimeter red dot glowered back.

Employing my weapon would be the easiest way out of the confusing hole I'd dug myself into. If I shot myself, Jack would have to process my remains. Handle my body. It would punish him, too.

Then I remembered that poor lance corporal in the public affairs office. He'd been pretty fucked up after taking snapshots of that kid on the stairs for the investigation. The kid had pulled the M16 trigger with his toe, or was it his finger reaching way down, with the muzzle under his chin? I pictured the PAO's photographer haloed by sunlight, all blue eyes and buzz cut, shooting my corpse with a digital flash. Who'd have to clean up the mess?

I got sorry and scared and clicked on the safety. Emptied and reholstered my weapon.

• • •

A few hours later, on my way to the head, I ran into Jack, who was on his way to regimental headquarters nearby. Seeing him filled me with relief.

"Come by before lunch," he said, "I've got a birthday present for ya."

I banged on his door just past noon. He closed it behind me, offered a chocolate pudding cup and a manila envelope labeled "T."

"I was going to get you the card from the PX that said, 'Happy Birthday, You're Eleven!'" he said.

I pulled out a mushy Hallmark card, entitled "To A Good Friend" in gold script. Inside was a manufactured poem I didn't read. Instead I concentrated on the ballpoint signature: "Jack."

In the manila envelope, Jack had included a DVD of *Sex and the City*'s first season, also from the PX. With the limited selection on our base, it was decent of him—he knew Marla and I often sneaked off to watch a few episodes.

We stood, and his arms wrapped around me.

"I found out when I'm going home," he said. "Just a couple weeks after you."

"That's great!" I said. "Birthday present for both of us."

"Yeah, no kidding," he said, "happy birthday. And no kidding,"—he paused, looked down at me—"I love you." He grinned. "So get in a better mood."

That night, after Staff Sergeant Garcia and I walked the now-protected fiber lines and I emailed an update, Major Davis called the SYSCON while I was in the head and said he wanted to talk to me. I frantically called back, but he didn't answer.

Soon Top found me. He said Major Davis wanted to talk tonight to go over the fiber run yet again. *What did I fuck up this time?*

I steeled myself to get yelled at. I was determined to do better. I had already hatched plans for improving the fiber run, organizing working parties in my head. *Ain't no party like a workin' party, 'cause a workin' party don't stop.*

I slunk nervously to the billowing tent where our company had its evening meetings. As I opened its heavy flap, something felt odd. There were more Marines here than just the major and Top.

"Surprise!" my Wire Platoon yelled, as Staff Sergeant Garcia led them in singing "Happy Birthday." They'd finagled an entire chocolate cake from the chow hall workers and stuck a blue chemlight in it for a candle. They presented me with a printer-paper card signed by all of them, even quiet Corporal Kim. Marla handed me a small packet. It was wrapped in orange tissue paper I recognized from the PX greeting-card aisle. I ripped it open to find a deck of the "Iraqi Most Wanted" playing cards. "So you'll always have your very own eight of hearts," she said. I fished out the eight of hearts, giggled at the Iraqi colonel's goofy smile, flashed the card to everyone.

I took inventory of the past few birthdays, all spent in Quantico. Twenty-one: Officer Candidates School. Twenty-two: the Basic School. Twenty-three: Communications Officer Course. Birthday number twenty-four—in Camp Taqaddum, Iraq, of all places—turned out to be the best birthday I'd had in a while, courtesy of my Marines.

Soon my troops retired to stand watch and play video games, sugar highs in full effect. I climbed to the roof of the SYSCON and lay down. The night quieted. Concrete chunks pebbled my butt and scraped the grip of my holstered pistol.

I wondered what that night would have been like instead, had

I shot myself that morning. Nitriles wadded in Jack's bunker. Dog tags unclipped. His troops briskly lifting a transport case. Jack slumped in a corner, maybe crying. Maybe not.

I shifted my half-full CamelBak under my shoulder blades, leaned back further, and exhaled. All I could see was black sky, full of brilliant stars.

TWELVE

Light My Fire

Redeployment Day minus One Week

A week before leaving Iraq, I shuffled through my postdeployment health assessment, a quiz to divine if we were crazy or sick or prone to shooting our loved ones. I gave the pasty navy doc the answers he wanted: *Yeah, I'm fine. No, I haven't seen anyone killed—lifting that transport case doesn't count. Yes, of course I was exposed to sand. No, no nightmares, not lately. Shit blows up, whatever. No anxiety, just stress. I'm an officer; I can handle it. Let me go.*

I was impatient with anyone who hadn't also been in Iraq for seven months, laying cable like my wire platoon. Our replacements' questions—where did this cable lead, when was chow, was there really a shot-up mural of Saddam Hussein—disrupted my precious workaholic routine, the one for which Marla had nicknamed me Rain Man. With the new troops swelling our numbers, we spent the next several weeks laying as much cable as possible. The Marines bore down, digging what trenches they could with a motorized Ditch Witch, then pickaxing the more sensitive areas bordered by concertina wire. They laid cables straight into sandy trenches, zip-tying them every few feet and burying them under fine grains. Their knees shone white, and they washed grit from their hands and necks before meals. It sucked, but it was celebratory for the Marines leaving country:

a last hurrah, the old guys willing to do anything to get out of there, the new guys excited to do anything at all. Even if it meant pulling cable hand over hand, fingers pruning with sweat in canvas gloves. As they tipped blue strands of Ethernet, bits of plastic tumbled to the ground, until everything was wired in. I watched Marla help dig, her slim figure bent at the waist, forearms dirty, red bun over delicate features. Though half the company comprised new troops, I didn't overhear anyone hit on her.

Fortunately, a squared-away comm-school classmate named Torres took over my wire platoon. Major Davis tossed me the keys to our battalion's suv, so Torres and I could inspect the cable line. Airfield to the left, headquarters to the right, the rest of Camp Taqaddum a desert plateau. The Euphrates winked below us if we craned our necks just right. Though I hadn't driven in seven months, the potholed roads felt familiar. Torres' clean uniform stood out against dusty upholstery.

I pulled over within sight of some junked Soviet planes, near a bunker where Marla had fucked Major Glory, and where I'd once gone on a long run with Jack and one of his sergeants.

Torres asked if mortars hit around TQ a lot. I told him that in the past month, most of the danger had stayed outside the wire. Except down that road—I pointed toward the gate where insurgents had crashed a vehicle full of explosives. And, I continued, when the mortars got close to regiment, peppered that empty tent—that was bad. Cut our fiber optics. Fucked up like a football bat. I climbed out of the car and kicked a toe in the sand, unearthing zombie cable. Torres didn't ask any more questions.

A few afternoons later, hopped up on caffeine with nothing to do, I called Jack from the SYSCON. He couldn't hang out; he had an angel coming in, he said, a mortar victim from Fallujah. All of the other times I'd been in his room, he'd shooed me away when the calls had come. This time, I asked to watch him work. I wanted to finally witness the cause of his sleepless nights.

"Major Davis would crucify me if I let you see this without him knowing," Jack said.

But when I asked the major if I could watch Jack work, he just braced a hand on the two-by-four door frame and said, "Yup."

In his bunker, Jack pressed play on *James Taylor's Greatest Hits*. It calmed him, he said. Two Marines lay a stretcher on sawhorses and unzipped a body bag: an ashen Navy Seabee with a fresh haircut. Blood sluiced to the sawdusted floor. One Marine held the clipboard; several more circled the body. They marked the locations of wounds and tattoos, crossing the Seabee's stiff arms over his chest for balance. Jack donned nitrile gloves and pulled a brand-new pack of Camels from the Seabee's pocket. A fist-sized hole bled where a heart had once beaten. *Fire and Rain* kept time.

I shifted from foot to foot as Jack counted dog tags, ID card, wallet, and photographs into a manila envelope. He motioned me back with an outstretched arm and a frown.

The whole process took only fifteen minutes. Soon the chaplain thumbed a cross on the Seabee's brow. The Marines put him in a fresh body bag, strapped it into a flag-draped transport case, and tied it tight with twine.

After, Jack wadded his nitrile gloves into the trash and led me to his room. We shut the door, no matter his Marines cleaning up in the outer bay. He pulled me in, kneading my back; I pressed my nose into his T-shirt and inhaled. Together, we breathed.

• • •

The next night, there were no casualties. I stayed long enough after midnight to hear Jack say my name and "I love it when you touch me" and his son's name and "I love you." He saw the dead when he slept. He thought of them constantly, he said, except when he was with me. We dozed an hour. Then I pressed my lips to his forehead, found my glasses, and slipped away. Six more days left in Iraq.

The next morning, on my walk to the SYSCON, I ran into Sanchez exiting the chow hall. I teased him about the samurai pads snapped to his flak vest: floppy hip guards, shoulder pads, a flat, triangular groin protector. Each piece sported a different pattern: digital desert, analog woodlands, Desert Storm chocolate chips. He was a Marine Corps fashion nightmare.

When I got to work, I found out the reason for all that gear. A VBIED had hit a convoy northwest of Fallujah, killing seven Marines and wounding six. A "mass casualty" event. Jack, Sanchez, and others rode out on a convoy to recover the bodies.

I couldn't sit still, so I walked into the TechCon van. Maybe the sergeants could offer distraction, whether with work, or with *Nip/Tuck*, their latest binge-watching addiction featuring plastic surgeons in compromising relationships. We watched for three hours, until we hit an episode where the plot revolved around infidelity.

I remembered that Jack was on the convoy.

This "other woman" had terminal cancer. Her adulterous lover helped her commit suicide before the cancer took her. The woman penned letters and sipped milk to coat her stomach while swallowing handfuls of pills. As she watched a lakeside sunset and the soundtrack played Elton John's *Rocketman*, I felt a wash of fear.

Jack was still on a convoy.

While watching the show, I wondered, *Will that be my punishment, too?* I'd become increasingly anxious about our imminent return to the States. Even more than getting caught, I feared losing what I thought was my only chance at love. Jack's wife in California loomed far larger than any bomb threat. A thick sludge of guilt coated my powdered-egg breakfast. I controlled my breathing.

He was still on a convoy.

After the episode ended, I stumbled out of TechCon into sunlight, blinking back lethargy from two hours of TV. I had to do something good, something officer-like: inspect the cable. Check on my troops. I controlled my breathing and swallowed the lump in my throat.

At the far end of the flight line, my Marines were deepening a trench in a spot plagued by heavy truck traffic. I walked the fiber optic lines along the airfield's edge, checking them for bald spots, kinks, and cuts. The air reeked of diesel. Helicopter rotor blades blended into a buttery hum. Sparrows flitted along eight-foot-tall Hesco barriers. After fifty yards or so, I stopped and peered down the flight line. Maybe a hundred yards left. Hot, boring work. I figured I could get to my Marines more quickly on the other side of the barriers, where there was a concrete path. I ducked behind them at the next opportunity.

• • •

WHUMP. Seconds later, a mortar landed on the airfield. I felt the blast wave in my chest and teeth. I took a few steps forward, thinking of my troops digging near the flight line entrance.

WHUMP. Another mortar round, a little farther away. A small rock kicked up by the blast flew over my head, or was it shrapnel? I had the urge to reach for it, to catch it, but I did not. Instead I turned around to head back to our company's headquarters. As my Marines fast-walked past me, carrying ammo cans full of tools, I thought only of counting their heads.

In the following months and years, I would wish I had been on the exposed airfield side of the Hesco barriers when the mortars hit, that I had sprinted full-tilt toward my Marines digging that trench, instead of taking a few steps forward before retreating. I would even wish I'd been hit by shrapnel, like a vigilant lieutenant. Was that the most fitting consequence of what I'd been doing with Jack? If he returned from his convoy to find me lifeless, would caring for my body have made him love me, made him stay?

In any case, he returned. Late that night, I lingered outside Comm Company's compound under a hard pearl moon. A hundred yards away, Jack's Marines unloaded one, two, three, four, five, six, seven body bags from their refrigerated truck. Then they hefted still more.

Under the floodlights, I made out Hoss's lanky silhouette,

spotted Mullins's round shoulders and rolling gait, almost heard his Southern drawl. Two more darted around the truck, its tailgate the height of their heads, shepherding paperwork. Sanchez stood straight and musclebound, lifting tirelessly. Sergeant Jonas barked orders.

Soon they all moved inside; they must have been grabbing clipboards and unzipping body bags. I stared at the bunker doors, wishing I could enter. If I had tried, Jack would have shouted me away, and Mullins and Jonas would have shaken their heads. I would like to say decorum held me back from going over there. Really, it was shame. The most honorable thing I could do was stay away. Wait to go home.

• • •

On my last night in Iraq, insurgents blew up our ammunition supply point. Though it was on the far side of the base, Jack and I still heard the familiar awful *whump* followed by erratic explosions. The mortars set off every round in our stockpile.

We'd been watching a movie in his room. As I shouldered my flak vest, he held up a hand. "Stay here; it's dangerous outside," he said. *Fuck off,* I thought, *I have Marines, too.* I flung open the door to his room and stalked toward the bunker exit. Before I could leave, Marla ran in, breathless and shaken, amid more explosions. She'd been outside when the mortars hit, and Mortuary Affairs' bunker was the closest place to take cover. She raised no hint of suspicion at finding me there. We phoned into the SYSCON, waited for a lull, and reported in person to check on our troops. The SYSCON was a blur of ringing phones, blinking lights, and Marines running in and out. We managed to count our troops quickly; most of them had been nearby in their tents, packing gear to go home. Even our comm lines looked okay—except, of course, the one to the ammunition supply point.

After the all-clear, while the sky glowed a steady orange, I went back to Jack's bunker, wondering if I'd ever leave TQ. The barracks close to the fire had evacuated, and so far there were no casualties. The Mortuary Affairs platoon would stay awake, just in case. Jack and I grabbed Coke Lights and scrabbled up the sloped roof. A couple of sergeants sat there already, legs splayed beside sandbags that still read, "No One Left Behind."

The hypnotic blaze faded to toxic smoke on a purple horizon. No one said much, just the occasional "damn." We stayed up there long enough for clouds to replace the cook-offs. We couldn't sleep, even if we wanted to. When the air chilled, we all clambered down.

Jack and I planted white plastic chairs outside his back door. We watched the glowing clouds and talked for hours: about Sebastian, about our plane ride to Kuwait, about the lecherous steward who'd insisted on calling Marla and me "princesses." Jack caressed the small of my back. We discussed plans for our weeks of postdeployment leave. None involved us together. When we heard a plywood door slam, Jack quickly withdrew his hand. Sergeant Jonas strode to the Porta-John. Jonas didn't say anything except "Good evening, sir, ma'am." Jack and I retreated inside, through his back door, and shut it tight. I figured I probably wouldn't get to hold him ever again.

Soon I dozed on his chest, and my watch beeped 0300. Even more than mortars, we feared falling asleep for his Marines to discover in the morning. I pressed my nose into his T-shirted shoulder and breathed deeply. He would fly home from Iraq three weeks later than I would. Reluctantly, I slid off his bed and took my glasses from their usual shelf. "Don't leave tomorrow without saying good-bye," he said.

Next day at noon, I pushed open Jack's nicked bunker door one last time. He waited in his black desk chair, understandably sleepy. He closed the door, stood, pulled me in for one last hug. He pressed his lips to my hair. "Being with you made this bearable," he said.

"Guess I'll see you at the ball," I said. The Marine Corps birthday ball, the mandatory-fun social event of the year, wasn't scheduled until November. It was the only time our paths were guaranteed to cross.

He said, "If I don't see you till the ball, I don't see you till the ball. But this is not good-bye."

I looked at him over my glasses.

His mouth softened, a hint of a smile. "This is, 'see you later.'"

THIRTEEN

American Girl

Redeployment Day

We spent a few days in Kuwait, going through customs and turning in ammo. Finally, Marla and I climbed the metal stairs to our U.S.-bound 747, shivering in the night. Out of habit, I followed her; she chose the very last row of economy before the toilets. Neither of us gave a shit about business class. I didn't want to talk. I did want to cry. The deployment had caught up with me, like a child after a long day. I slumped into the gray upholstery, closed my eyes, and feigned sleep.

Despite having yearned to fast-forward the past seven months with my daily internal mantra of *I want to go home*, I felt no gratitude at liftoff. I didn't want my time on TQ to be over; I wanted to be back in Jack's room. When I closed my eyes, our final night together replayed in my mind.

When he'd opened his black belt's Velcro, I didn't wince and bolt, as I might have months earlier. He'd grabbed my hips with sureness and rolled me onto my back. I'd felt his solid weight atop the length of me, through thin layers of cotton and nylon, as we'd kissed. He'd shimmied down, face even with my fly, tugged at my trousers, peeled down the grayed Under Armour. A haze of touch and moisture. His ultimate request, my ultimate refusal; we'd taken it as far as I allowed. I wanted to be back there, though, for those minutes I'd dozed on his chest. I had felt a powerful peace with him, safety I'd rarely felt anywhere else.

I checked my pocket for a pen, anxious to write every detail of the previous night in my journal. But with Marla sitting right next to me, it would have to wait. She sighed, no doubt thinking of Major Glory. Every feminine motion of hers irked me— which was ironic, considering the thoughts swirling in my head. Each minute we breathed the plane cabin's stale air took us farther away from the desert. I cursed every scratchy flight-crew announcement; gentle turbulence felt like rockets. When Marines staggered to the bathroom, their hands on my seat-back jolted me from thoughts of Jack.

We stopped to refuel at Ramstein Air Base in Germany. I crossed the terminal, stomping blood through my clotted calves, and shut myself in a metal bathroom stall. Old paint flaked from the wall; the latest coat shone hunter green. As my trousers hit the deck, I looked to my right and saw a roll of one-ply toilet paper. Gone was the need for the ziplock stash of chow-hall napkins in my cargo pocket. I choked up with relief. From here on out, there would always be toilet paper.

After shuffling and seat belts and more airline food, our plane's wheels touched down in California. I landed with an inner scream. I banged down steel stairs onto concrete and stumbled through a receiving line of elderly veterans. Six of them had come out to shake our hands as we debarked. They wore red USO jackets and yellow-ribbon pins. I submitted to their wrinkled grips, feeling unworthy of their respect. On a table in the terminal lay an assortment of cell phones for Marines to call their families. I didn't call anyone. The USO cared for us well, but I wanted none of it. It would take me two days to call my family.

On base I smelled the beach as we waited to turn in our weapons. The air felt liquid, compared to Iraq. Everyone else in the desert-camo queue jiggled with anxiety. They couldn't bear the delay until they saw their spouses, who waited for us a ten-minute drive away. But I didn't mind. There was no husband, not even a boyfriend, waiting for me. The closest substitute was back in Iraq and married to someone else. My roommate Nell and my childhood friend Maddie would meet me at the parade deck. After sliding my pistol through the armory's barred window, I felt naked.

We rumbled to the parade deck in a white government school bus. I blinked into afternoon sun as my boots hit the asphalt. A crowd of balloon-holding, sign-wielding families surged toward us: a human rainbow exploding after seven months of brown and gray. A corporal from Data Platoon, sunburnt beneath a white-blond buzz cut, kissed his girlfriend. Nell jumped out with flowers, startling me, but I appreciated her enthusiasm. Behind her stood Maddie, the one who'd lamented in a letter that she couldn't send me a vibrator. I hugged them both. Together, we searched the rows of seabags for mine. I tottered under two, a walking mountain of ripstop nylon.

As Maddie walked me to her Honda, she offered McDonald's chicken nuggets and a snarky giggle. "So, what's his name, Jack?" she said. She'd read my mind. As I buckled my seat belt, I said, "I shouldn't worry about this, right?"

She paused, gripped the Civic's stick shift, muscled it into gear. "Nah, man, don't worry about it," she said. And in the New York brogue of our childhood, echoing our weary mothers as they'd kicked off tight pumps after another day crunching shoulder pads against Wall Street suits, she shrugged, "whaddaya gonna do?"

I had no idea what I'd do. I didn't yet know that my workaholic stoicism, punctuated by spirals into shame and self-condemnation, obscured just how common experiences like mine were in war. And it would be years before I learned the term—moral injury—for combat-zone transgressions of deeply held moral beliefs.

I acted on instinct my first evening back, unhooking my seabag's clasp alone in my room. I hadn't bought any furniture yet, so I sifted through my pile of camouflage and laid out my unwashed green sleeping bag. I cued *Fire and Rain* on my laptop, lay on my back, and closed my eyes, sniffing my gear in vain

for the desert. My civilian belongings felt alien, with one excep-
tion: I curled up in that sleeping bag with my old pink blankets.

• • •

We all sat through a week of mandatory health screenings and
readjustment seminars—don't-drink-and-drive and don't-beat-
your-spouse and welcome-home speeches and paperwork. I
slouched, knees wide and arms folded, in the freezing base the-
ater, and took the lectures no more seriously than the navy doc's
questionnaire on TQ. My nightmares—buckets of bloody limbs—
wouldn't begin for another two months. And I wasn't about to
admit my feelings of massive guilt or breathe a word of my surprising longing to be back in a Groundhog Day routine, where
contractors fed me and washed my laundry, where I could stand
my SYSCON watch blindfolded, and where I was ten minutes'
walk from Jack. He felt like the only person with whom I could
talk about Iraq. I knew I'd see him again in November, at our
battalion's formal ball for the Marine Corps birthday.

I didn't call my parents right away. My official excuse was
that my cell phone had died while I'd been gone, and it took a
couple of days for AT&T to mail a new one. But the real reason was that I relished this time alone. When my family asked
questions, I felt something akin to emotional asthma, unable to
explain the depth of my feelings for a reality they'd never encoun-
ter. There was no way they could understand the satisfaction
of a successful fiber optic repair job, the backslapping vibe of
an evening brief, the weight of a transport case, or the surreal
beauty of white smoke in an orange sky. Their questions—"are
you glad to be home?"—only grated on my nerves. Yeah, duh,
I was glad to be home. But I also felt a surprising nostalgia for
a vibe I couldn't quite put into words.

My roommates understood. Nell and I lived with Lani and
Becca, logistics officers I'd known several years. Sweet, peace-
able Becca's Naval Academy cheerleading stint complemented
her degree in robotics, and I'd known strong, outspoken Lani

since we were nineteen-year-old midshipmen training in the Mojave Desert. They both had just come home from Iraq as well; we'd served on different bases for the same seven-month span. Becca had led hazardous convoys. Meanwhile Lani had stood watch in a tactical operations center on a base that had suffered heavy mortar and rocket attacks. We relayed only the facts of our deployments, never emotions. One evening Becca, Lani, and I were fixing dinner when a door slammed upstairs. We jumped, then sheepishly avoided eye contact, remembering we were in California. We didn't speak of it afterward.

Instead we basked in the backyard of our four-bedroom condo: a lemon tree, a round picnic table, and scads of bougainvillea. Every time I washed my hands, I marveled at running water a mere ten feet from my bedroom, grateful I didn't have to tromp through sand to a Porta-John.

Our expeditions throughout greater San Diego felt like *Sex and the City* meets *Jarhead*. My roommates gladly got mani-pedis, trotted around in sandals, and ran spandex-clad on the beach. Away from the deployment microscope, they elicited no commentary or judgment and could appear both feminine and strong. Plus, they were much less emotive and boy-crazy than Marla had been.

I took comfort in their sisterly presence at home, grateful for their invites to turbo kickboxing classes and margarita nights. Still, I rarely joined them. I wore the same baggy T-shirts and skate shoes as before leaving for Iraq, and gave no sign of what had happened during deployment. I was afraid they'd think less of me if they knew.

My roommates never questioned my lack of interest in girly frills; they'd always known me as a nerdy tomboy whose ammo pouch passed for a purse. But I was even quieter and more reserved than the odd girl they must have remembered. Although I'd known them for years, I couldn't bring myself to confide in them. So I ate frozen yogurt and laughed, and I pretended that I was fine, that desperation, guilt, and grief didn't patter a relentless drumbeat in the back of my head.

Most Marines lost weight while deployed, but I lost five pounds after returning. Every morning I woke up anxious. I tried to relax, but couldn't: no matter where I went, whether beach, library, or restaurant, as soon as I sat down, I wanted to be somewhere else. Song lyrics jangled my car speakers: *riot girl and she's angry at the world* and *she will be loved* and *I'm finding out that true love is blind.*

One Saturday I woke at six thirty, drove twenty minutes to Oceanside's beach, and ran for half an hour on packed sand. Then came my reward: the unoccupied skate park. No one was there to laugh at my wrist guards, thick kneepads, and helmet. I dropped into the six-foot-tall ramp and lulled my thoughts into a rhythm, forgetting everything in favor of kickturns. Waves crashed on the beach, and my anxiety finally subsided. As my legs pumped the board up and down, I thought, *I can do this for another day.*

I went to the near-empty supermarket four times in one day, just because I could, wandering dazed amid the produce. Four years later, *The Hurt Locker* would make this type of scene a cliché, but I wasn't as confused as veteran stereotypes would have one believe. That afternoon I was simply happy. Back. Alive. Speakers wailed a Muzak version of "Total Eclipse of the Heart." I wanted to ride the unwieldy cart past eye-popping displays of perfect bananas, fresh greens, and red peppers. Instead, I slowly maneuvered it through the air-conditioned aisles, marveling at bright packages of processed foods. I couldn't decide on a single brand, but it didn't matter—everything looked so clean, so bright.

My car became my sanctuary, locker room, and storage unit; I found calm in motion. On one drive home through suburban streets, "Accidentally in Love" piped through the radio, and I remembered humming along to it in the shower trailer on TQ. I sang, bounced in my seat, and thought of Jack. *This is what love must feel like*, I thought. *I'm in love.*

Though I'd changed profoundly since leaving Carlsbad earlier that year, the village had remained the same. The pizza place near the beach still added artichokes and pungent feta to its pies, while the New York-style joint down the block still seasoned its slices with perfect oregano flecks, just like back home. Tom Giblin's, the local Irish pub, remained raucous on weekend nights. The overly air-conditioned Mexican restaurant served the same enchiladas, while impassive bungalows hunched near the art deco seawall. How could everything have stood still for seven months, when I now felt so jarringly different?

I missed Jack's voicemail on my new blue Nokia at work one morning. He'd just returned from a convoy. An IED had exploded in front of the lead vehicle; some of his Marines had been up front. "It was pretty touch-and-go there for a while," he said, "but we're all back safe in the barn." And they finally had a date to fly home.

I listened to his message twice, standing in a breezeway outside Comm Company's Camp Pendleton office. Amid blue sky, car washes, and polished supermarket fruit, a message from Iraq teleported me into another world—one that, emotionally, felt sharper and clearer than the easy reality I now occupied.

I commandeered an empty office, closed the door, and pressed an elaborate number sequence on the government landline's backlit keypad. As a CommO, I knew the U.S.-Iraq dialing instructions and had memorized Jack's number. The eleven-hour time difference made it evening back on TQ. He was flabbergasted when he picked up the phone. We spoke for twenty minutes about how his Marines were doing, the date of their return, how I was adjusting back to California, how he still couldn't believe I'd called, how he'd sleep well that night since he'd talked to me. He said little about the IED. After hanging up, I hid my grin. I didn't know what kind of euphoria or heartbreak would await me in the following months, but I wanted no questions from colleagues about the person on the phone's distant end.

FOURTEEN

Falling

I took three weeks of postdeployment leave, the military's version of paid vacation, penciling my social schedule in my tiny green notebook from Iraq. The intense itinerary spanned Maryland, where I'd see my mom, stepdad, and brothers Dave and Zach; New York, where I'd see my dad and extended family; and finally Boston, where I'd see my brother Matt and friends from college.

Mom picked me up at BWI with a big smile and a soft-sweatered hug. Her celebratory exclamations embarrassed me; they reminded me of when we were small and came home after a week at our dad's, when she'd had enough time away from us to miss us. In spite of the resentment I'd harbored in Iraq, I was glad to see her. Dave hugged me, slouching in his jeans; he needed a haircut, and his eyes were kind. "I convinced her to leave the balloons in the car," he said. *Balloons. Christ.*

It was a half-hour drive to Silver Spring, and Mom's two-footed braking-accelerating unsettled my stomach. "What do you want to eat, honey?" she said. "Chinese food?"

"Sure. Whatever. Haven't had Chinese in a while." I batted balloons out of my eyes.

We picked up the food and headed home, to a house where I hadn't grown up. Zach barreled into me. He was taller, probably about the same size as Jack's son, Sebastian. My stepfather was there, too, but he didn't say much to me, nor I to him.

After dinner, Mom made me tea and sat next to me on the couch. "You okay?" she asked. Her gray-blue eyes softened.

She tried to hug me, squishing me close against her. "My glasses," I mumbled, and shifted out of her hold. Human contact, even with my own mom, could make me cry, so I remained guarded. I didn't want to look weak, didn't want to tell anyone about deployment. Least of all her. Where had this focused attention been when I was a kid? I didn't want her to know about me now.

I looked away. "I'm fine," I said. "I'll show you pictures."

I opened the photo files, folders nested in folders. A giant grasshopper. A stomped camel spider. The Ditch Witch for digging cable trenches. Jack popped onscreen, wearing scrubs and a grim expression. "Mortuary Affairs. That was rough on him," I said, clicking quickly past.

Mornings, I ran down wooded trails in Mom's suburban neighborhood, leaving a Post-it with an estimated return time. I darted down dirt paths, removed my socks and sneakers, and cooled my toes on the creek's pebbled bank. Physical exhaustion gave me brief moments of peace. Still, Mom worried. I usually returned half an hour after the Post-it said I would.

I spent hours in her basement, rooting through boxes from high school and college. Neil Diamond cassette tapes. David Duchovny wall calendar. The pizza box on which I'd learned trigonometry, its equations still sharp in blue ink. Forever ago.

From the crawl space, I heard my phone's voicemail chirp, and I gasped. I'd missed Jack's call from Kuwait. His message played through the tinny connection. "We leave tomorrow morning," he said, sounding spent and relieved. I replayed the message, knowing I wouldn't be there after his plane landed, when his bus rolled onto base. His wife and son had the right to that scene; I didn't.

Mom said her church had prayed for me every Sunday. Zach

and my stepdad (who'd grown up Jewish) sang in the Lutheran congregation's choir. Their religious choices confused me; I hadn't grown up Lutheran. But I passively sat through church in a raglan baseball shirt with a USMC seal spattered across the front, bought by a college buddy for fifty cents at a thrift store. My hair, still damp from the shower, flew away from my face. The congregation's "thanks for your service" and "welcome back" embarrassed me. Mom's hand firmly gripped my bicep. I startled each time she grabbed me, flinched when she hugged me from behind.

When the service began, the female pastor, stacked spheres of round belly, bosom, face, offered us blanket forgiveness. Afterward I stopped her in the lobby. "So, I can just say I'm sorry and be done? I don't have to tell anybody what I did? No confession?"

"That's between you and God," she said.

Are you serious? I think. *Do you know what I've done?*

And what had I done, really? Well, possibly destroyed a family. Conduct unbecoming, prejudicial to good order and discipline. All traded for a few strokes, ego and otherwise. Back in my mother's car, I didn't feel at all absolved. Rather, guilty and frustrated—I neither had a guarantee of Jack's reciprocal desire nor the courage to let him go.

He called me the next chance he got, from the same cell phone-littered USO table I'd ignored upon touchdown in California. We hadn't seen each other in a month, but we chatted for less than a minute. He said he just wanted to hear my voice. We said little else; how do you translate staring over a phone line? And I knew he'd be with his family soon.

On Amtrak between DC and New York, I made another flowchart.

Yeses, nos, diamonds, decision points, subbullets. *If he leaves her in the next year. If he leaves her in the next three years. If I find somebody else. If he stays with her. If he waits until Sebastian turns eighteen. If he waits until Sebastian's thirteen*—the same age Jack was when his parents split up.

If. Maybe. When?

If Jack stayed in California, how long could I wait for him? I considered graduate schools. Could I go to Caltech? UC Irvine? USC? Maybe I could get into Caltech, earn a PhD in physics, and be an understanding stepmom. I didn't realize I was trying to replicate the stepfamily I'd grown up with, in an effort to change the ending to that painful story. I hadn't yet learned that families morphed and grew on their own timeline, that no calculation could engineer the life-path I craved. I had to build my own, from the bottom up, by living it. But I didn't yet know that.

As the train pulled into Penn Station, I remembered I needed to wait two years until I could get out of the Marines and have a say over my own life. These weeks of approved leave marked my only free time; the Corps still owned me.

Uptown, I visited a physicist grad-student friend and met her PhD adviser. Their chatter about particle physics and the Large Hadron Collider comforted me. When the professor encouraged me to apply there in a year, I hitched up my jeans and nodded. Columbia's neoclassical architecture seemed like a peaceful oasis in the cityscape.

. . .

I traveled north to my dad's house upstate. He welcomed me with pineapple upside-down cake, his preference, not mine. The TV was on as usual, tuned to cable news.

From his black faux-leather recliner, he believed in only his version of my war. He parroted the conservative party line, squawking about the most recent explosions in the barren landscape from which I'd just returned. "I know. I was there," I spat back, and turned away from the TV. He bragged about a commercial weapons lubricant—Milspec—supposedly better than the military's standard-issue cleaners. He railed against the generals who wouldn't supply it. He, of course, knew better. He rehashed a newscast featuring a father (not him) who had mailed his son a pallet of Milspec. I flashed back to my brothers and me, three small heads in the backseat of a Dodge, Dad shaking Matt by the shoulders when he misbehaved. "Your father provides for you," he'd said back then, impotent rage caged in his jawline, complaining a breath later how child-support payments bled him.

I figured he would have loved for me to deploy again, for Matt to deploy, too, for anyone but him to do the fighting. "Waste the bastards," he said, as airstrikes blared bright-green onscreen. He sipped Sam Adams, glassy-eyed, and growled again, "waste 'em."

Dad asked me no questions about my deployment, and I told him nothing.

I stalked away for dawn runs, my only time alone. Wild turkeys gobbled through red fallen leaves. I loped around neighborhoods that used to be familiar. My mouth dried; my temples ached. I wondered if Jack was running, too, in California. Five miles later, I slipped back through the screen door, kicking off my sneakers on pilled raspberry carpet. Dad waited, impatient at the breakfast table. Nothing brightened him more than feeding us. "Okay, eat now," he said, assaulting me with eggs, cereal, coffee, piles of bacon. Sweaty and thirsty, I ignored him, filled a tumbler with water.

I mentioned the wild turkeys I saw, said we should shoot ourselves dinner. "No!" he said. "You can't do that here!" He did not own a gun. His version of roughing it, he liked to brag, was the "Holiday Inn without cable." He chomped chicken tenders at the mall food court, fried calamari on the stove, slurped sweet sherry. He was soft, paunchy America.

I picked at the bacon, stood, and sipped coffee. He pushed bowls of nuts at me, salvos of misfired love. I hissed in Italian, "Lasciami stare!"—leave me alone!—and stomped off to shower. When I looked back, he sat deflated. Only then would his eyes soften with concern. Maybe he was even afraid of me.

Then I felt guilty, which was worse than pissed off. This look on his face, I remembered. It was there when my mom divorced him.

• • •

In Boston, my brother Matt flew in for a weekend he had off from Air Force training. As I hugged him, I caught a faint whiff of Old Spice, a glimpse of chest hair under his collar. He wasn't the kid toting his overnight bag beside me on the way to Dad's car, or even the teenage cadet running in formation with our ROTC buddies. He was a lieutenant himself now, a grown man.

We didn't talk much about my deployment; instead, we discussed his first few months of training and his adjustment to full-time military life. Over barbecued-chicken pizza, he said, "by the way, you're the executor of my will."

"That works," I said, "because *you're* the executor of *my* will."

"I am?"

"Dude, I *told* you before I left for Iraq! If anything happens, look in the green backpack!"

"What green backpack?"

"The green backpack where my will is!"

"Glad we didn't need that," Matt said.

I told him nothing of TQ or Jack, instead concentrating on the skate parks and beaches in California, how cool it was that our backyard had a lemon tree. We parted with hugs; he went to get beer with his own college friends, while I watched a Sox-Yankees game from a friend's couch. Late that night, a voice-mail alert blipped on my phone.

"Hope you're having a good trip to Boston," Jack said. We hadn't spoken in a week. "You're probably out drinking. Anyway. I've been drinking. Just called to say I hope you're having a good time, tell you I miss you, wish you were here. Goodnight, beautiful." He paused for a ragged breath. "I love you."

I doubled over, shocked and delighted and aching.

•   •   •

My return to Camp Pendleton brought a new assignment as the sole communications officer for Maintenance Battalion, far north on the base. There, twelve hundred wrench-turners supplied ammo and fixed heavy equipment, trucks, and electronics. My new Marines had just returned from a different base in Iraq than the one I'd been on. None of us would deploy again anytime soon.

Plaques, medals, and sheaves of manuals lined the walls of my new battalion commander's office. The stern, driven lieutenant colonel was married, with four school-age children. "Got any kids?" he asked me.

"No, sir."

"Married?"

"No, sir."

He grinned, and his eyes twinkled. "Then you're ready to deploy again!" I could tell he was joking, but I had the inkling that going back to Iraq might be less complicated than living stateside.

In the following weeks, I spoke little at staff meetings, trying to fit in. I knew a few of the other officers. And I had a section of only eight Marines, not twenty or thirty. The job seemed manageable.

The few friends back home whom I'd told about Jack had said I should give him up. Though I'm not proud of it, looking back, I called his cell phone every few days. Over the next few weeks, I learned to tell his drunk voice from his sober one. Drunk, his voice sounded fluid and yawning. His sober voice was shot through with remorse or crisp brightness, depending on his mood and whether he was on his way to get drunk again.

He offered to take me to a weekday lunch on base. After weeks of missed calls and email delays, we settled on a Monday. November clouds tamped down California sunshine. I parked behind his platoon's warehouse, not hiding, but not out in the open, either. I walked through aluminum bay doors, past a line of green containers bearing nuclear, biological, and chemical protective gear. I shook hands with Sanchez and Sergeant Jonas for the first time in a month, *how you doing, life's good, yeah, it's great to be back*. There was Jack, standing on industrial carpet in green-and-brown woodland camouflage. I had never before seen him in anything other than a tan desert uniform or scrubs.

"Hey," he said. Same dimpled smile. He was taller than I remembered.

"Hey." I smiled bigger than I probably should have in front of his Marines.

As we walked to my car, he said he was short on time, had to be in a general's office in half an hour.

"That's okay. We'll just go for a drive." At the wheel, I snuck glances his way, elated and hopeful. But after more than a month of terse phone calls, of storing up things to say, we strained for conversation. I couldn't just blurt out, "So, you gonna leave your wife for me, or what?"

Instead I jerked my head back toward his shop. "How's everyone doing?"

"Oh, you know," he said, "the usual."

At least one of his Marines had gotten a DUI their first weekend back. Another was getting a divorce, but they'd all known that was coming. Half of them took psychotropic medication. They all had nightmares. One still wet the bed.

"I'm sorry," I said. I didn't know what else to say.

"It's not your fault," he said. What he didn't say—but I remembered—was that he thought the fault was his. He had volunteered the platoon for mortuary affairs duty in the first place.

He navigated me toward the Fallbrook gate, past the munitions depot, toward firing ranges, and farther, avocado groves. He pointed to the parking lot for the Sidewinder, a small luncheonette. As we pulled into a parking space, we checked the dashboard clock. He had twenty minutes left—no time for lunch.

"We can sit here a couple minutes," he said.

I asked him how Sebastian was. Jack said he was great, talked his ear off all the time, like had to get it all in before Jack left again. Jack kept trying to tell him he *wasn't* leaving again.

First weekend back, he said they could do anything Sebastian wanted. Disneyland, Legoland—anything. Sebastian wanted to go camping.

"I was like, fucker, I just spent seven months camping!" Jack said.

I asked what they wound up doing.

"We went camping," he said.

Jack had forgotten how much Sebastian's pet guinea pigs screamed in their cage. He slept on his boat at night, but drove back to the house every morning to take him to school, had dinner with him, and tucked him into bed every evening.

I raised an eyebrow; he was living on his boat? By himself? But I didn't want to ask; we were finally having a good time.

He apologized for not seeing me sooner, told me of awards ceremonies for his Marines. He himself was about to be awarded a Bronze Star.

"That's why I have to go to headquarters today," he said. "I didn't want to do it in front of the whole battalion."

Of course not. Jack, who wanted to put our entire deployment behind him, didn't want a formation in his honor. Just a short, no-frills ceremony with the colonel and general and a few other officers there. If you minimized awards proclamations and summaries of action, you dodged resurfacing memories. I imagined few Bronze Star awardees wanted to mull over what they did to earn them. Like a good Marine, Jack steered clear of glamorizing what he'd done in Iraq—a job that existed only because others had died. He refused to honor himself above them. He'd brought all of his own troops back alive, a true reward—and deep relief—for any unit leader.

Soon our time was up. I drove him where he needed to be. When I pulled over, he laid the fingertips of his left hand on my right knuckles. Then he put on his cover. "I'll see you at the ball on Friday," he said. I looked away as he climbed the stairs to the brick building.

As I drove through winding hills back to my unit, stomach in knots, I thought of all the questions I hadn't asked.

FIFTEEN

Semper Fidelis?

Camp Pendleton, California—Redeployment Day plus Two Months

That week was the Marine Corps birthday ball, the social high-light of the year for every unit. Celebrated since the 1920s, the formal event involves a marching color guard, speeches, a birth-day cake sliced with a sword, and the same bugle calls Marines have known for generations.

Jack and I would attend not one, but two of the same birth-day balls. The first, at the officers' club, was for commissioned officers—warrant officers and above: a couple hundred Marines and their dates. Back in Iraq, Jack had mentioned that his wife always came to this one. The second, a week later, was for the battalion we'd deployed with. Jack had said his wife never came to that one; instead he usually got shitfaced with his troops.

I'd loved the excitement of the ball since I was an eighteen-year-old ROTC midshipman. My dress blues' skirt and tailored blazer fit well; I'd kept off the weight I'd lost. I put on pearl ear-rings and ensured my newly earned medals—one for deploy-ing, one an award for doing my job—were neatly mounted on a thin metal bar pinned above a breast pocket.

The night of the officers' ball, the thought of meeting Jack's wife pricked my stomach with fear. Marla picked me up in her small green sedan. She was still dating Major Glory, but he lived far away, flying with a reserve unit back East. He'd join us the following week, at the battalion ball.

The O Club lobby teemed with Marines wearing gilded medals, high leatherneck collars above, swords swinging below. Marla disappeared to chat with some other officers. I headed for the bar and ordered a Sam Adams.

Behind me, I heard the slow *pock-pock* of shoes on polished tile. A familiar voice boomed, "Are you old enough to be buying that beer?"

"I might be," I said, turning around to face a chest full of shiny metal: Gulf War, Global War on Terrorism, Bronze Star. My first time seeing Jack in dress blues.

"Hey," he said.

"Hey."

"I'll just be a minute," he said, hustling down the hall and ducking into a small conference room. Marla was in the doorway; she motioned me over, jerked her head inside. When I looked in, I saw a photographer snapping a posed photo: Jack and his wife flanked by flags. She was ten years older than me, tall and elegant. She wore a silver Cinderella ball gown and elbow-length gloves, platinum blond hair piled high and ornate. Ringlets cascaded past her eyes. In her satin heels, she was only slightly shorter than Jack. He stood stiffly, bracing one arm around her waist. He did not smile as the flash erupted. My stomach felt like lead, and I muttered, "You gotta be fucking kidding me."

I was jealous, of course. She was gorgeous. But I also judged him for preferring her. He wanted some princess in a ball gown and stilettos, mincing down the hall? I'd never be her. Here I was in my sensible uniform skirt, low-heeled shoes, and Harry Potter haircut. A few medals, sure, some silver bars on my epaulets— but if who he really wanted was the belle of the ball, well—that would never be me. I was a warrior.

I didn't stick around to chat.

A few minutes later, they sat at their table, safely across the ballroom. I took a chair beside Major Davis, my back to them.

My eyes swam as a CD player bleated adjutant's call, and the color guard marched on to start the ceremony.

After the speeches, I picked at my dinner and traded pleasantries with Major Davis's wife. Jack bought me and the major Coronas, planted the bottles in front of us, and patted our backs, all buddy-buddy. The last time he'd touched me, his hand had brushed my knuckles; before that, a chaste good-bye hug in Iraq. The time before that, his tongue had been between my legs.

I barely acknowledged him, pounded my beer, and got up in search of another.

After dinner, I wandered back toward the dance floor, but stopped short of trespassing on the parquet where Jack's wife danced the Electric Slide. I usually danced drunk, but loaded as I was, I wouldn't be dancing here. On another badly timed pass, as Shania Twain sang "Still the One," I glimpsed Jack swaying with her, a thousand-yard stare on his face. I spun on my Windex-polished heel and wove down the hall. Marla stood in the hallway, ready to go. I assured Major Davis that she was driving, certainly not me. As we left in her car, I remained silent about how I felt; I'd confided in no Marine so far.

Half an hour later, we spilled into the after-party at Tom Giblin's, the Irish pub off base typically teeming with junior officers. I felt grim and deflated and ready to drink. Amid hooting lieutenants and loud guitars, I downed rum and cokes, to zero effect. I stood on the outskirts of conversations spoken above my half-nodding head. I didn't care whether I heard. I couldn't get drunk enough to blot out silvery gloves and platinum curls— more hard evidence that frillier women triumphed in matters of the heart.

On some level, I must have guessed Jack would never be fully mine. He had, after all, chosen to keep up appearances in his marriage. But I'd grown so used to slinking around in the romantic background, catching what attention I could, that I made the cognitively dissonant choice to hold out hope.

The Headquarters and Services Battalion ball, the Marine

Corps birthday celebration for the battalion we'd deployed with, was held four days later. I drove an hour through Temecula canyons to a casino hotel east of Camp Pendleton, one of the few local places that could handle all eight hundred Marines. Sagebrush snapped in the November wind. I braved the cold in a tight black tee shirt in hopes Jack would spot me crossing the parking lot.

I'd mistaken the ceremony's start time, so I slipped in after dinner started, scanning the room. We saw each other across the ballroom floor. He smiled, and my gut spiked with ice. Instead of his wife, he'd brought his old buddy Carl; they'd been lance corporals together in the Gulf War. After the meal, we all shook hands over Jack and Cokes. Carl's rented trousers had been hemmed six inches too short: unintentional tuxedo capris. Mullins, still a reservist, had flown out for the weekend from his home in Alabama. Major Glory slipped an arm around Marla's shoulder; she gave him a lipsticked smile. I sipped and reminisced with them and did not even pretend to want to dance. Here we stood, beribboned and shiny, all together again. But it felt a few degrees off, like a summer-camp homecoming with more caged tension. I kept a constant bead on Jack's location.

After the festivities ended, my heels clicked on polished faux marble as slot machines clanged in the background. The lights shone high, but smoke curled higher; Marines slurred into courtesy phones, shouting at their buddies upstairs to *come down, have a drink, where are you, which girl?*

"Wanna see our room?" Jack asked, Carl by his side. "We got the honeymoon suite; it's ridiculous."

Carl laughed, his eyes twinkling, as I followed them back to their room. He was the only person Jack had told about me. I felt excited, intoxicated not just by our drinks but by this dangerous proximity to Jack. At the same time, I felt safe with Carl there, at least until he started packing to leave. He would drive home to his own wife and daughter an hour away.

"Make the room stop spinning," I murmured, holding Jack's elbows as Carl zipped his jacket into a garment bag.

"It's okay," Jack said. "I like it when you hold me."

That last shot of Crown Royal, I thought, *was a bad idea.* Whatever happened, I'd blame the booze.

Still holding Jack's elbows, I tugged his sleeve. "Walk me back?" I said. Jack nodded at Carl and followed me to my room, where I ducked into the bathroom and threw on pajamas. I could barely stand straight.

"Nice jammies," he said, in the tone of a babysitter. I knew he was trying to do the right thing, and I figured I should, too. We said good night, not touching, barely meeting each other's eyes. "I'll come check on you later," he said, "after Carl leaves." But Jack had made promises before.

I lay in bed, paralyzed, sick at the thought of him gone. I didn't know when I'd see him again. *So that's it,* I thought. *That's what I waited two months to see him for.* I hadn't had the courage to ask him anything in the car the previous week or to confront him about his wife at the ball. So many other people had been around. I didn't know when I'd get a chance to tell him anything again.

Like the gamblers downstairs, I gave up and threw all-in. I wrangled on pantyhose, skirt, too-loose undershirt, button-down blouse, stupid red tie. Manhandled pearls back into pinholed earlobes, jerked smooth the medaled jacket, touched the keycard still in the hidden pocket, stepped into shiny uniform heels, and strode up to the room number I'd memorized. He was out of uniform, bluejeaned and polar-fleeced.

"Lookit you!" Jack said. "What're you doing up? I was gonna come check on you!"

I didn't know if he really would have come.

"I wanted to say good night," I said. He followed me back to my room. We'd had just enough scotch; no stopping the train wreck this time.

As we wrapped each other in our first solid hug in months, he said, "I didn't see you during the ceremony. I was worried you might not come."

"I jacked up the time on the invitation," I said.

"Last week was weird," he said.

I was surprised he'd mentioned the awkwardness of the officers' ball. "That was really hard," I said.

"I'm sorry." He breathed into my hair.

"Are you drunk?" he murmured.

"Sober enough to know what I'm doing. You?"

"I know what I'm doing."

I looked up at him. "Do you love me?" I said.

"You know the answer to that."

"Well, do you?"

Gripping my shoulders, he met my eyes. "Yes. I love you." He brought his mouth down on mine.

Afterward, he spooned my back, wearing a wet towel. Neither of us was quite awake, though I could stay up with him till the world ended. I turned and murmured, "No matter what happens, we'll always be friends, right?" He held out his little finger in response. Pinky swear.

It was more than I ever anticipated happening, but for me it would never be enough.

Less than an hour later, red numbers blinked 5:35. "Someone could see me leave. I gotta go," he said. He pulled stonewashed jeans and crumpled fleece from a chair. One last kiss. He closed the door, and the latch flipped home. My adrenaline drained all at once. Alcohol leached from my pores, leaving a twinge of hangover nerves. Had to be at my new battalion in three hours.

I showed up late to my office in the back of a dilapidated warehouse, my venti latte the heaviest weight I could stand to carry. My new Marines, eyes glued to their computers in the outer office, didn't notice. Still wearing jeans, I shut the sliding door to my office and curled up in a wheeled desk chair. The stained carpet rippled as I rested my boots on a second chair. By noon, my headache had cleared enough for me to put on my uniform.

I tried to wall the previous night from my mind, but flashing images seared through. I might as well have carried a chow-hall plate of powdered eggs and brittle toast; it felt like those mornings-after in Iraq.

That evening, after work, the gravity of what we'd done seeped in. I took panicked breaths. The goody-two-shoes lieutenant in my head knew this was punishable under the Uniform Code of Military Justice. And not only had I betrayed these values without the thin excuse of falling mortars, here it became even clearer that I was helping to undo a family. I cowered, sweatered and jeaned in my swaying loft bed. I'd staved off guilt before, but now it felt like I was falling.

I palmed my phone, thumbed his number. The call went to voicemail. Once again, he'd evaporated.

I waited a few minutes, dialed his number again. This time, he picked up. "I'm . . . not . . . okay," I said, and my halting voice cracked.

"Can I call you back in ten minutes?" he said. "I need to get to a place where I can talk."

I paced my room, turned the phone ringer up as far as it would go. I wasn't convinced he'd call back, until he did.

"How are you feeling?" he said.

"Not so good," I said.

"I have about fifteen minutes," he said. "I'm in the car. I told her I was going to Staples to buy a desk." I winced at the mention of his wife. He'd moved back into the house when the weather chilled, burrowing into a basement man cave. Now he slept there.

"I don't know what I'm doing," I said. I feared pressing Jack for answers. I didn't think I'd like what they'd be.

"I love you," he said, but he didn't say more. "If you need me, call me. I'll call you right back." He assured me that I was okay—an assurance that, at the time, I couldn't conjure for myself. Then he said, "I'm at Staples. I'd better come home with that desk."

As he drove home to his wife and his son, I slept alone on cloud-print sheets in a kid-sized loft.

The following week, I drove to Jack's office to meet him for lunch. In the car, full of adrenaline and sideways anger, I sang along with Green Day. *American Idiot* had been my only album purchase after Iraq, purposely subversive. The lyrics lambasted foreign policy—*I'm not a part of a redneck agenda*—a welcome reminder that I could, at least secretly, ditch the Marine party line and connect with life outside the Corps. I thought if I set my speakers loud enough during the forty-minute drive, if I sang my tone-deaf heart out, that I could rally enough rebelliousness to stave off self-recrimination. For a few minutes, I rode high on guitar chords, optimistic I could someday rejoin the civilian world. My bravado evaporated as soon as I reached Jack's office. I shut down the engine so quickly that I forgot to turn off the radio, guaranteeing the music would blast when I got back in.

Jack sat behind the desk in his red-carpeted office, ensconced in shelves of memorabilia: plaques and framed certificates and his Mickey Mantle autographed baseball. We nodded to his Marines, like our going to lunch was no big deal.

I slid into the buttery upholstery of his new Passat. In following years, I would think I spotted it everywhere, straining my eyes in vain for the yellow "Marines" sticker across the back window. He'd bought it with some of his deployment money. Hadn't consulted his wife. I remembered him at chow on TQ, counseling Sergeant Jonas to "talk to Momma" before buying a new motorcycle. I raised my eyebrows, shrugged. Up to him to follow his own advice.

We ate at the luncheonette where we hadn't had time to go before. A single waitress staffed it: Kim, fiftyish, bleached-blond hair with dark roots, gold nametag, pink lipstick, toothy grin. That fall and winter, Jack and I ate there together enough that Kim would recognize me even without him.

After she penned our order on a green notepad, we stared at each other, transported back to Iraq, breaking the silence with stilted questions. Jack asked about my new job, mentioned he'd met my new battalion commander at senior staff meetings. He asked if I'd heard from Marla. "She's okay," I said. "Not sure if

Major Glory's gonna work out. The distance, I guess." I picked at what passed for a salad: iceberg lettuce with fried chicken bits and honey mustard. Mealy, bland tomato slices. Torn strips of processed cheese. His burger looked much better. I stole a few of his fries, dipped them in ketchup. Our fingers shone with fry oil. We stared some more. "This is just like the tea garden," he said.

The bill didn't top twenty; Jack paid. It felt like a date, though it was early afternoon and Marines and retirees surrounded us. Before leaving, I checked my reflection in the bathroom mirror. In my baggy camo, I looked barely old enough to date anyone, least of all Jack. A handy appearance for hiding whatever this quasi-relationship was.

When I returned, he was already standing. "Come on. I'll drive you back." Already I mourned the loss of him for another afternoon, a week, maybe a month.

Before starting the car, he brushed my salty fingertips with his own. I saw specks of dirt by his eye, raised a curled index finger, wiped them gently away with my knuckle.

"Listen, I had a great time the other night," he said. His eyes looked saggy through his sunglasses.

"Me, too."

There was a long pause. He reached for the emergency brake.

"I'm in love with you," I said.

He exhaled sharply.

"So we should probably confine our friendship to lunch," I said.

The dreams started in the following weeks. In one, I sat on top of a picnic table, balloons tied to it, cake nearby. Sebastian ran around kicking a soccer ball. Jack sat by me. His wife walked slowly uphill, toward us. I woke up breathing hard.

• • •

Out of ideas, I went to confession. I hadn't envisioned this at Mass back in Kuwait before our convoy, fighting back tears while the priest sang "Be Not Afraid."

In a Catholic church in Carlsbad, I sat face-to-face with the South Asian priest. At first he misunderstood my halting words, and in a gentle accent encouraged me to marry and start a family with, as he put it, "this boyfriend." When I explained that Jack was already married, the priest immediately directed me to stay away. Use my conscience. The flesh was weak.

As penance, I drew five Hail Marys and five Our Fathers, a light penalty. I briefly considered shaking the priest by his vestments. *That's it?* I wanted to scream, much as I'd thought with my parents' Lutheran pastor. *Don't you know what I've done?* I said the prayers and stayed through Mass and wondered if God gave extra credit.

As the oldest kid in my family, I'd always resented the story of the prodigal son. The older son had never been rewarded, I'd thought, for following the rules. Now I'd become the prodigal one. As the exit hymn ended, I did not feel at all absolved, but at least I didn't feel worse. I had at least tried to make amends.

Over a decade later, I would learn the definition of moral injury from a National Guard counselor's online brief—"perpetrating, failing to prevent, bearing witness to or learning about acts that transgress deeply held moral beliefs and expectations," which "results in highly aversive and haunting states of inner conflict, turmoil, and shame." In a writing class, I'd learn the mantra, "You're only as sick as your secrets." Telling my story—public confession—would, in fact, light the path to shedding my burden. But none of this was at all clear three months after deployment.

• • •

A few weeks later, on Christmas Eve, I stood duty at Force Service Support Group Headquarters, wearing woodland camo and a Santa hat. Mercifully, the office received no calls of DUIs or arrests, just a couple of Red Cross messages for Marines who already knew their bad news from home. When I drove home from watch Christmas morning, my roommates had long departed, either for deployments or holidays with boyfriends and far-off family.

I saved my sole package until that groggy afternoon, a FedEx envelope bearing a Brooklyn return address. I opened the cardboard zip-closure and gold-green-red wrapping paper to find a copy of the *Bhagavad Gita*, a gift from my literary uncle and aunt. On the flip side of a shiny Tannenbaum, the card read:

> Perhaps you will think this is an odd choice for a Christmas present—and, perhaps, you have already read it.
>
> My guess is that you are struggling still to absorb your experiences in Iraq and your time in the Marines. I know that you do not want to worry any of us, especially your mother and father, but, in your heart of hearts, please, please acknowledge to yourself what you truly feel. Lying to yourself is the road to madness.
>
> This book is about dharma, variously rendered as "duty," "law," "custom," and about 15 other meanings. In sending it to you, I hope a non-Western view of "why it is we do the things we do" (also a possible meaning of dharma) will help you gain a little perspective. I do not think the answers to life's hard questions are necessarily found in books, but I hope this helps a little.
>
> Merry Christmas from your Aunt and Uncle whose love for you is not dharma, but a privilege allowed us.

As I read it, a lump started up my throat. Lying to myself was the road to madness. But how could I admit the truth? I read a few verses of the *Bhagavad Gita* and soon fell asleep, crammed on the couch with white pillows.

SIXTEEN

Worst Christmas Ever

Carlsbad, California—Redeployment Day plus Three Months

I picked Mom up from the airport the day after Christmas; she'd volunteered to fly out for the long weekend. She reached for me, her brown hair in a long bob, a hot-pink sweater across her shoulders, enveloped in her signature vanilla moisturizer. I allowed myself to be hugged and willed myself to smile, even as she furrowed her brow with concern. She didn't press me with questions, for which I felt grateful. We tried to do mother-daughter things.

In the Best Western's breakfast room, the Samoan guy pouring my coffee fixed me with a long, friendly smile. "Hey, you're cute," he said. "Even without makeup."

"Low maintenance," I said.

"Men like to hear that," he said.

I wandered toward the rack of pastries and white bread, inspecting the Lucite bagel container for trapped flies. Something familiar strained through overhead speakers. Guitar chords. It wasn't—oh fuck. Yes, it was. Something swift and needling pained up my throat, which was suddenly dry. *In my mind I'm gone to Carolina*, James Taylor crooned. *Motherfucker.*

I set down my empty Styrofoam plate and walked outside to a wood-planked deck. *Just a couple of minutes*, I told myself, blinking back tears. The air felt chilly; I pulled my sweater sleeves over my thumbs and fingers, paced the deck, rocked from my heels to my toes. Brushed away tears with my knuckles, wiped my nose on my sleeve like a preschooler. Wished I'd brought a paper napkin outside.

Behind me I heard a sliding door. Mom. I ducked away, rubbed a wrist at my forehead. Just needed some air. Yeah, that song.

"Oh, James Taylor." She rolled her eyes. "I know, I don't like seventies music either. You'd think they could pick something better!"

"No, I mean—" I swallowed hard. This might shut her up for a while, maybe. "They played it in the Mortuary Affairs bunker when they worked on the bodies."

"Ohhh." A whisper. Taking it in. Fake understanding, because who could understand? Gentle hand on my shoulder. I twisted away. I didn't want to be hugged. I didn't meet her eyes.

"You want me to check if it's over?" she asked.

I nodded. Yeah. Like when I was seven, hiding under a chair during the scary parts in *Pee-wee's Big Adventure*. She went back inside.

In a minute she waved from the sliding door, smiling, trying not to look worried, trying to get me to smile, too. "C'mon, let's eat," she said.

Afterward, I drove her downtown, where we stopped in every frou-frou gift shop. She looked at postcard portraits of Frida Kahlo. "I want to buy some stickers," she said. "They'll motivate me to write in my journal."

Christ, if you want to write, just write in the fucking journal, I thought, stalking the store. The shelves held crystals. "Spiritual" new-age baubles. Stationery rotten with flowers. Old-lady girl-power crap. Mom stopped in every gift shop in downtown Carlsbad, chatted with each owner, invariably a middle-aged woman. I scanned a dozen versions of Frida Kahlo's unibrow and unsuccessfully searched the rubber stamps for my name. These stores—they were all the same store, I thought, anger rising. The menopause store. *When I am an old lady, I will wear*

a purple dress and a red hat and fuckall it won't matter, because
I'll just be a man-less biddy celebrating the unique flower of my
life until I die like the rest of them. I heard the Muzak and looked
at the stained Sheetrock ceiling, thinking of Jack. Where was
Jack? He hadn't called. No Merry Christmas? I walked outside
so my mom couldn't see me cry.

She found me in the driver's seat of my car, shoulders as high
as my ears, head resting lightly on the steering wheel so as not
to trip the horn, tears muddling the pleather cover and stain-
ing my forearms. She had a small bag with her; she'd finally
bought her stickers.

"Heyyy, hey, what's the matter?" she said, soft, as if I were a
wounded animal. She reached out and tucked a hank of hair
behind my ear.

"Just some guy. Some dumb guy," I said.

"Oh, honey. In Iraq?"

"Yeah."

In a flash I was a junior in college again, breaking up with
my first boyfriend, admitting this to her through the grimy
receiver of my dorm phone, holding it away from my mouth,
so tears couldn't drip on it. I remembered staring at my dorm
room's thin carpet, thinking I would never be loved again. I
knew I had been wrong then, but the feeling returned with a
vengeance. I was twenty-four years old and convinced I would
never be loved again.

I emptied my nose into a fast-food napkin and put the car
in gear. There was no way I'd tell my mother any more details
about Jack. I didn't trust her not to probe my reasons for wanting to be with him, or to unearth that he was married. I didn't
want her to draw parallels to her own situation sixteen years
before, when she had left my father and taken up with my stepfather. I worried that learning of my transgression might lead
her to expect forgiveness for bringing my stepfather into our
lives. Even six years after leaving her home, I wasn't ready for

those conversations. And no way would I let her offer opinions on how I lived. Jack, I maintained, was none of her business.

Her suggestion of a nap sounded good, though. At home, I climbed up to my loft and slept. When I dropped her back at the airport the following day, I hadn't told her anything more, and she hadn't asked further questions. And though I wouldn't admit it at the time, her presence did make me feel slightly more patched together.

SEVENTEEN

Wintry Mix

With my roommates deployed or working long hours, I welcomed company. One January afternoon I fell in love with a blond, mellow Californian: Buster, a six-year-old Labrador retriever. I led him from the shelter with a length of rope, and we raided Petco for collar and leash, toys, and a fluffy bed. When he hopped out of my Toyota, dog hair covered the backseat. I didn't care.

Buster made the rounds of our house's first floor and nestled on his new bed. He already knew how to sit and shake hands; he didn't bark. The following days and weeks marked a new routine, one in which I poured bowls of kibble and threw rawhides instead of ruminating on my worries. I found trails and parks in which to walk him, sometimes with friends, but mostly just the two of us.

Sunday mornings, Buster waited at home while I played two hours of pickup ice hockey at a mall forty minutes away. In college I'd played in a recreational league but had never been particularly talented. Nervous about getting hurt, I blasted Good Charlotte and Blink 182 on the drive to psych myself up. At the rink, I kept my head down and spoke to no one. Most Sundays I was the second-worst player on the ice—new players seemed to show up every time—and went hard for the puck, probably too hard, milking extra seconds of ice time until I gasped for breath. Once I took a stray elbow to the jaw. On the drive home, shivering and sweaty, body aching, legs sore, I'd feel completely physically spent—and calm. Then I'd shower, let Buster outside, take Motrin if needed. Posthockey naps marked the few times I found peace.

• • •

In late February my dad planned to visit, but a snowstorm kept him in New York. I hadn't seen Jack in two months, but emailed him anyway, offering the two minor-league hockey tickets I'd bought. "The game's tomorrow; take the tickets, take anyone you want. I wasn't really planning on going. Take Carl, take Sebastian."

He called my office phone. "How 'bout we just go together?"

When he called again the following afternoon, I figured he was bailing.

"What time can you get down here?" he said.

I threw on jeans, blue skateboard shoes, and a formfitting gray sweatshirt. Got in my car and parked behind his shop.

When I entered his office with its mounted awards and autographed baseballs, his Marines had all gone for the day. He didn't close the door before he hugged me.

Sunset painted rainbow hills near Temecula as he drove us north on I-15. Cold wind whipped against the windows. Jack held my hand while we talked. It had been five months since I returned from Iraq, three months since we'd driven separately to the casino nearby, not knowing we'd wind up in that hotel room until we did.

He'd recently learned he had orders to Quantico, Virginia. Across the country. He'd leave in a few months. His wife and son were moving with him. Eventually he would get a divorce, he said; it was a matter of when, not if. Then he sighed, said I'd probably be married and pregnant by then.

"No," I said. "No way."

We arrived at the game sometime during the second period. He took my hand as we crossed the parking lot, but I let go, shaking my shaggy head. It felt too strange—what were we? Old war buddies or something more?

Inside the arena, the home team's mascot was a bulldog, same as the Marines. Jack bought me a hot dog and water, ordered himself a bratwurst and a Pepsi. After we'd eaten, he said he had to go to the bathroom. It was about nine o'clock, likely Sebastian's bedtime. *You don't have to lie to me*, I thought, *to make a ten-minute phone call home.* This felt like cheating. It *was* cheating. I made no mention of his overlong absence when he returned, just curled into my oversized windbreaker. In the third period, the mascot danced over to our seats and tousled my hair, as if I were a little kid. He must have thought Jack was my dad.

But we remained glued to those thinly upholstered chairs, shivering, happy to sit next to each other, despite our private worries. I asked Jack how things were at home. I wanted him to be all right. And I wanted to gauge my chances.

He said that ever since he'd made it home from Iraq, he couldn't stop thinking about how much his life sucked. He still slept in his basement man cave. He wasn't excited about Quantico. They had a buyer for their house in California, but he didn't want to buy another house with her. This last bit gave me a jolt of guilty hope.

He said Sebastian, of course, was a terrific kid. Couldn't catch a baseball to save his life before he'd deployed; now he could field anything. Wednesday nights, Jack usually took him to an arcade or to the movies. Some nights Sebastian's mother took him out. And sometimes, Jack said, they did stuff all together.

The "all together" part threw me. However bad he claimed his marriage was, he'd kept it together. He could build a life around it, whereas I felt like I'd left my personal life—the part I cared most about, anyway—back in Iraq. My hours with Jack were a clear detriment to his family. But if I could no longer spend time with him, how would I truly return from the desert?

I wondered if my mother and future stepfather had these conversations before they dismantled my childhood family. Did my mom tell him how she tied smocks on us before we finger painted, or how Dad taught us to pedal bikes, or about their nightly preparation of three small bowls of macaroni? How once in a great while, they'd let my brothers and me jump on their four-poster bed? Did the mention of children give my future stepfather pause, or was my little family already doomed?

The arena's air horn sounded; the game was over. We drove past scrub-dotted hills in silent darkness and returned to Camp Pendleton around eleven. My adrenaline bled away. As we pulled up to his office, he asked if I wanted to come inside. Of course I wanted to. I stuffed down worry about prying eyes and blinked back exhaustion as he flipped on the fluorescent lights.

We sat on the couch in his red-carpeted office that smelled like him, surrounded by shadows of plaques given to him by adoring Marines. Come daylight, we'd be locked back into our respective roles. We probably wouldn't see each other for a while. However much I hated that seesaw, at the time, I accepted it. I didn't see any other way. He held me and nuzzled my neck. I knew that to let him touch me was the surest way for me to keep him there. But the sooner he got what he wanted, the sooner he would leave. Better for me to leave first.

Before I drove home, I let him sweep me up in one knee-buckling kiss.

• • •

Redeployment Day plus Six Months, California

A month later, Jack offered to bring Sebastian to watch my pickup hockey game on a Sunday afternoon. I thought this was progress, though whether in a romantic or a friendly context, I wasn't sure. *He still might not come*, I thought, but I wore a white tank top under my gear. I skated circles before the game, quieting my spiraling mind.

On my next-to-last lap I heard whistling from the balcony. Jack and a small boy—it must have been Sebastian—in their coats, watching. I shot, missed a wide-open goal. Fell down after the game started.

As the shifts rotated, we players slid down the benches, elbowing each other through cold, smelly gear. Thus armored, I'd never had more than a four-line conversation with any of these pickup teammates, though I'd played several months of Sunday-afternoon games. Typically, I frowned with a lowered gaze, but that day I felt light and happy, and glanced up to the balcony every few minutes. The end of the game couldn't come soon enough.

When the buzzer sounded, my tight helmet had left a red mark on my forehead. I pulled off my jersey and shoulder pads and sat on the bench, freezing. Baring my shoulders in a tank top felt risqué. I kept my shin guards and skates on, wanting to prolong the act of undressing in front of Jack. I figured he and Sebastian would come down at any moment to say hello. After twenty minutes of shivering on the plastic bench, when the last of the hockey players had lugged his bag up the escalator, I slid down my ripped hockey socks and un-Velcroed my shin guards. Itchy heat bumps sprang up on my legs.

On the way to the car, I phoned Jack, thinking maybe I'd missed them; maybe they were having lunch in the food court upstairs. "We're at Toys 'R' Us," he said, a half-hour drive up the freeway. "Sebastian and I had some things to do. I'm getting him one of those Lego Technic sets." They'd only stayed ten minutes at my game.

I countered the familiar hollow pang of disappointment with the knowledge that Sebastian deserved as much of his dad as possible, especially since Jack had been deployed half his life.

"Here," Jack said over the phone, "talk to Sebastian."

Wait, what? Sebastian?

"Uh—hello?" I said.

"Hi!" Sebastian's adorable kid-voice, earnest and bright.

"So, you're at Toys 'R' Us?"

"Yeah."

"Whadja get? Legos, huh?"

"This Lego Technic stuff. They have these little spider dudes that turn into motorcycles." Or trucks or helicopters or tanks, whatever fashionable Lego he didn't yet have.

"Whoa, spider dudes. That sounds pretty cool. Do they have the little wires you put in to make them robotic?" I said.

"Yeah." He handed Jack the phone a minute later. Motorcycles. Helicopters. Spiders. Awesome. But I wouldn't meet him that day, or ever.

Instead I drove alone back up the highway. Buster licked the salt from my shins. The heat rash took a day to fade.

Seventeen years prior, Dad had tried to buy us off, too, mistaking toys for love. Valentine's Day, when he and Mom had been newly separated, he'd left things for my brothers and me on our flagstone doorstep. Small boxes stacked three high: candy. And atop the pile, just for me, a doll. Face, feet, and hands buffed porcelain. Painted blue eyes, black eyebrows, red lips. Blue gingham dress and white pinafore over a cotton body.

But instead of pleasure at the extra gift, I'd only felt embarrassed and guilty. I hadn't wanted special treatment just because I was the only girl. With special treatment came pressure to *be* special, to be extraordinary, to deserve it. *Blend me back in, let me be one of the boys, let me disappear*, I'd thought.

I still thought that maybe, if I agreed to stay invisible, the same agony I'd felt in my family—the simultaneous powerlessness and obligation to make sure everyone around me was okay—would fade. If I came in second, Sebastian would grow up safe and loved, with his dad around. On the other hand, now, if Jack left his wife for me, I thought I could build a better stepfamily than my parents ever could. I understood what it was like to be at the nexus of family wars, to have a parent try to buy love. I knew how to treat a kid, how not to demand what they could not give. Sebastian, a sweet little guy, would be all right with me. I liked hockey and T-ball and Legos, too.

I didn't know then that until I made peace with my past, my present would hurt in much the same ways as before.

EIGHTEEN

Good-bye?

Carlsbad, California–Redeployment Day plus Seven Months

My loneliness flared on a Friday night early that spring. After dinner, I wound up at Giblin's, the officer hangout, for a captain's going-away party with colleagues from my new battalion and their spouses. Marla wasn't there. She would soon deploy with a civil affairs group, something that suited her much better than communications. I wore my going-out armor: low-slung jeans and a karate T-shirt, an outfit I'd later discover prompted strangers to ask my friends if I was gay. I felt too exposed wearing anything glittery or revealing. The Irish guitar band started low and lilting, then rose to a roiling pitch, and I bobbed my head to the music. I never went so far as to dance on those loud nights.

Jack, of course, wasn't at Giblin's—he was with his wife and son, getting ready to move. In the meantime, I knocked back two White Russians and finished my first-ever Car Bomb. It tasted like chocolate milk. I finished my second one on a bench next to a fellow communications officer. In the middle of a professional analysis of our networks, I turned from him with an abrupt, "Excuse me, I have to go vomit now."

In the miniscule toilet stall, a buddy's wife cleaned up after me. Two more women steadied my shoulders and steered me to the door. No one in our crowd was fit to drive. Another captain friend, Walker, lived within walking distance of the bar. I stumbled a few blocks behind him down cracked pavement. He was one of my CommO big brothers, and I trusted him. Inside his cottage, he pointed down the hall. "If you're gonna puke again, bathroom's over there," he said. I shook my head and wiped my mouth. He pulled aside a pillow on the tan suede sofa. "Here ya go." He lurched into his room, nursing his own buzz. I spent the night in jeans and T-shirt on his couch, in fitful drunk sleep.

I didn't throw up again until the morning. I wet a washcloth and pressed it to my neck, feeling water droplets cascade down my shirt. My head pounded with dehydration and shame. *Classy, T. Now you're the girl who puked at the bar.*

Walker was waiting in the kitchen, rumpled and T-shirted, when I came out. "Heard you boot. You okay?"

I nodded, ashen-faced and thick-tongued, and asked for aspirin.

He fed me his last two Tylenol and brought two glasses of water to the living room.

I set two slate coasters on the coffee table and sat on the sofa, putting my elbows on my knees and head in my hands. I was trying to press away the headache and keep tears from spilling. I accomplished neither.

I hadn't told any fellow Marines what had happened in Iraq, or about my ongoing rumination. I figured if anyone found out, I'd make *all* female Marines look bad, like the young female lieutenant who got filmed having sex with a pilot. Or the *ho* from my old sergeant instructor's *bitch-dyke-ho* speech. Or simply someone who couldn't hack a deployment. And there was always the chance I could have been court-martialed. I felt ashamed for having let my feelings compete with the job I'd been called to do. Why did I get to live, when others had died? If I'd resisted Jack in Iraq, I could have returned with my head held high, proud of completing our mission. Instead, no matter how technically proficient or well liked I'd been, I had this mark on my conscience. That day, I thought I had no choice but to suffer from my actions.

But I'd known Walker for several years; he'd been married and divorced, and was now in the midst of another painful breakup. Maybe it was this fissure in his captain's armor that made me feel safe enough to tell him the truth.

"It's a guy," I said. "It's stupid. It's wrong." I started crying from more than the hangover.

"Officer?" he said, sniffing trouble like a pro. I nodded.

"Married?"

I looked up. Jesus, the guy was good. I nodded nervously. "Yeah."

Head hanging, I spilled out my story. I wanted to crawl under the sofa. Every few minutes I paused, sipped water, and waited for an ass-chewing. A stern, "you should have known better." Hell, maybe even a punch.

More than court-martial, I feared gossip. I didn't tell Walker Jack's name. I was pretty sure they didn't know each other anyway.

But to my surprise, Walker responded with compassion. He didn't condone what I'd done, but he wasn't about to turn me in. It was Jack's fault, too, he said.

"And T, you have to realize, if you were really that important to him—"

"Yeah?"

"He'd leave his wife."

•   •   •

I asked Jack to coffee in May, two months after he and Sebastian had stopped by my pickup hockey game. Within weeks, he would move to Quantico. His Marines had thrown him a going-away blowout at Hooters the night before.

He waited at a picnic table outside a downtown Starbucks. He half-stood to greet me, holding a frozen macchiato to his forehead.

"Sergeant Jonas stopped the car to let me puke last night," he said, squinting, then added, "you look great."

"How you doin'?" I said. I couldn't help wanting to hug him, but I didn't move.

"I'm doin'," he said.

Parents walked screaming toddlers past us, and he winced at the noise.

"You want to just go to my place?" I said. Then after a beat, "I don't mean, like—"

"I know," he said. He tossed his full drink in the trash.

When our garage groaned open, my roommates were gone. Buster trotted to us, tail wagging, and Jack knelt and cooed. He petted him for a long time, grabbed his collar as if to steal him.

"My dog," I said, queasy and grim. I slid open the backyard door, let Buster do his thing.

"Does he sleep with you?" Jack asked.

I shook my head no.

"I was gonna say, lucky dog."

"No, my bed's lofted. Wanna see?"

"Sure," he said.

"I don't mean—"

"I know," he said.

He followed me upstairs. I hoped my underwear didn't show above my low-rise jeans.

I led him to my tiny room, its lofted bed, night-sky sheets, and SpongeBob SquarePants minicouch.

"Of course," he said, "This is *your* room."

He wrapped his arms around me in a hug, then pulled back, still holding my elbows. Didn't try to kiss me.

"You look great," he said again.

"I love you," I said.

"I love you, too."

"So if things are ever different—"

He sighed.

"If things are ever different," I said, "let me know. Until then, I have to move on."

"Are you seeing someone?" he said.

"No!" I said. "No."

Downstairs, on his way out, he bent down with a smile and again hooked Buster's collar with his finger.

"My dog," I said again. "Haven't you taken enough?"

He looked at me, opened his mouth, said nothing. Put on his sunglasses.

NINETEEN

Paddling like a Duck

California, Redeployment Day plus Nine Months

Mornings that year at Maintenance Battalion, I woke from nightmares about Iraq. Bodies and gore and guilt bubbled beneath conscious thought as I ran the ridgeline of trails behind our warehouse at 0615, showered in the grimy head at 0705, and sat behind my desk in uniform by 0730. I never wore headphones; instead I listened to my thudding footfalls, my rushing breath, my occasional whimper. Dodged piles of whitening coyote scat, while meaty-haunched rabbits bounded through bushes. I glimpsed white tail-puffs and translucent ears amid wild baby's breath. Dew soaked my sneakers; knobby pine scratched my shins. I ran past the burnt dregs of Santa Ana fires; hollow reeds and green seedlings sprouted through black loam. Pollen and thistle and wildflowers meant summer.

By the time I pounded down the mountain, my lungs burned, and my cheeks were tear-stained, but I'd bled off enough sorrow to get through the rest of the day. Pain eliminated pain, or so I thought.

Fridays I brought Buster running. His head bobbed and tongue hung out as his doggie legs worked up steep inclines. His back formed a compass needle nose-to-tail. He sniffed the air to dash after rabbits, and once, a deer triple his size, its hoofbeats sure on tufted shrubs. His yawping joy made it worth the sprint to catch him after he ran off.

We'd trot back to my office, both panting, Buster limping. He'd slurp water and slump belly-down on the cool concrete of the supply cage.

Work numbed me just enough to get through the day; instead of ruminating over my failures, I could concentrate on reacting to network outages, staff meetings, and endless accounting for laptops and hard drives. No one could criticize me for this diligence.

After three months without contacting Jack, I convinced myself I'd outrun him enough to look back.

In late July, one year after his birthday kiss, I dropped him an email with false nonchalance: "Happy birthday, old man. How's life in Quantico?"

It was a Friday, so I pushed the slipup to the back of my mind and joined two new female-lieutenant friends for a last-minute foray to a San Diego rock festival. We arrived in time to hear the night's final song: the Killers' "Mr. Brightside," whose lyrics haunted me all the way home. I returned alone the next afternoon to sing under my breath to Dashboard Confessional—*don't say that everything's working when everything's broken*—and bought a pink, slim-fit Killers T-shirt, one of few cute garments I'd own.

Assigned to the shooting range the following Monday, Tuesday, and Wednesday, I woke at 0345, drew my 9-mil pistol from the armory, and practiced all morning. Twenty-five yards from the bench. Fifteen yards standing, isosceles stance. Then kneeling. When my thumb stretched to slide the safety off the Beretta, its red dot winked back. I dropped my magazine to the ground, knelt, reloaded from the pouch on my left side, fired more rounds. The muzzle's clean pop was a joy.

I had never failed to qualify expert with the pistol. But as the week progressed, I stewed with nerves at Jack's lack of reply. Emailing him the previous Friday had been colossally stupid,

I thought. My shame and remorse felt permanent, doubly so at his nonresponse.

Midweek at the range, I wedged in earplugs, clapped on big earmuffs, and blew through the pistol course. Blue sky and sun belied my mood.

At the end of the day, we made sure we carried no extra bullets. The junior Marines grabbed at each other's cargo pockets, a cursory show of conscientiousness.

But I was an officer; no one checked me. It was also my privilege to leave early, spared the task of policing spent brass from the cracked concrete.

I fished in my left hip pocket for my car keys. There I found one more bullet. I left it in my pocket and walked to my car.

This was illegal, removing live ammunition from a Marine Corps shooting range. But I figured I hadn't exactly been a poster child for honor that previous year.

It was, however, perfectly legal for me to transport my weapon back to our battalion. I slipped it into its holster, nestled it into the back of my Matrix, and rumbled down dirt roads, ruminating. *Shouldn't have sent that damn email,* I thought. How shamefully desperate, to telegraph that I missed him. No matter how much running and working and concertgoing I used to paste over the past, Iraq's memories chased me down. *I just can't look, it's killing me,* the Killers had sung the weekend before.

I parked the car in my usual spot in front of our comm building, down the street from the armory.

When I swung open the car door, hot summer sun blazed. A breeze hit, all sagebrush and sharp chaparral. My carpeted office, first-lieutenant's warrant in its plastic sleeve, and eight data-crunching Marines all stood in the building ten yards away. I closed my fingers around the bullet in my pocket.

I wanted to take my pistol in its familiar green holster—the same holster I'd worn in Iraq—up into the ridgeline. To the top of the hill I'd climbed for PT runs and hikes. The same trail I ran with my dog and my Marines, where rabbits hid.

I thought, *Maybe I should hide, too. Forever.* I was an officer with no integrity. Who couldn't get her shit together enough to not run after a married guy who didn't love her anyway. Who would fuck things up for all the women in the Corps, if anyone learned her secret.

I couldn't keep up this charade of having my life together. I thought it would be better if I just left. I wanted to hike to the top of that hill and put a bullet through my head at four thirty on a Wednesday afternoon.

I opened the hatchback, pulled my pistol from the trunk, and slammed the door. Smoky wind shivered through weeds.

I imagined the resulting slim hole, blown-out exit wound, coyotes lapping my brains. My body felt not my own as I veered toward the path to the ridgeline.

At the time, my Marines would have been packing up for the day, arguing over whose car they'd change the brake pads on, who'd kick whose ass at HALO in the barracks, the speed of one lance corporal's Honda del Sol.

My boots quickened on hot asphalt, and I held my weapon tighter. It would mean an end to all this pain. I thought of my birthday in the SYSCON the year before.

I looked up at the trail to the hill, gray against brown earth and cerulean sky.

Would my Marines hear the shot? Which of them would hike up and find me? Who would take care of my dog?

The dog.

Who *would* take care of my dog?

Who was going to feed the dog?

I had to feed the dog.

I had to be home for Buster.

I turned away from the ridgeline and shuffled to the armory before I could change my mind. I slid my pistol butt-first to the unsmiling armory clerk. I waited until she turned around before tossing the bullet into the amnesty box.

I kept the radio off on the slow drive home. Through the sliding glass door to the backyard, Buster napped. When I shoved the door aside, he shook off sleep and trotted over, angling for a neck-scratch and some kibble. I grabbed his scruff and pulled him close and nuzzled his velvety ears.

Four days later, Jack responded: "T, Thanks, I feel very old. . . . how's my dog? . . ."

• • •

A week afterward, on my twenty-fifth birthday, Jack's old Marine Sergeant Mullins shot into a noisy crowd. The incident made national news.

I still had the ambulance company business card he'd slid into my sweaty hand back in Iraq. I dialed the number, left a message, and paced the backyard, ten feet from the lemon tree. My birthday barbecue was slated for later that afternoon; Buster begged for gristle I scraped from the grill. Potato-chip salt dusted my pink Killers T-shirt.

When my phone rang, Mullins's drawn-out vowels blotted out the California sun, plunging me back to the night that our ammunition supply point burned. He said he was holding up, trying to keep his wife and kids out of the media fray.

"Sanchez or Temple been in touch?" I asked. I couldn't help it.

"The Sir's trying to come here as soon as he can," he said.

My pulse sped up. The same man who'd rested a hand on Mullins's tattooed shoulder and written him up for awards would of course drive the ten measly hours.

After that, there wasn't much to say.

"If you need anything, Mullins, anything at all, you call me, you have my number," I said. "Next time I'm back East, I'll visit."

I never did.

Instead I drank and plastered on a jokey mask for my buddies and their families. I chatted with a talkative, dark-haired captain. I shoved Mullins and Jack to the back of my brain as a friend's toddler fed Buster Cheetos.

In the following months, images of both of them filtered

through: a magazine photo, a quote from Jack, the shirt Mullins wore to his arraignment. Jack, of course, spoke on his behalf. Though Mullins's controversial act had made the news, his worth as a Marine had never been in doubt.

My sins were far less dramatic and public, but I had spent a year fearing a firestorm of judgment if they ever became so. It took a long time, but Walker's compassionate counsel, combined with our Iraq comrades' understanding of Mullins, opened a new possibility in my mind: I was worth standing up for, too.

• • •

That summer, I explored my surroundings in fits and starts, haltingly riding the skate park's concrete lines. On my riskiest nights, I eschewed dorky pads, but despite looking slightly cooler and sticking tricks more when people were watching, I made no friends there.

I saw other young women skate only once, on a day I'd cut out of work early. A long-haired blond girl landed several tricks on a six-foot ramp. She looked at me with curiosity, saying nothing. Near her stood a few teenage boys, and I marveled at their kickflips, maneuvered in torn sneakers and baggy cargo pants. Postchildhood, prebeer-belly, the boys had peaked in athletic ability—twinned with peak jackassery. They ripped armpit farts, snuck cigarettes, dared each other to ollie higher. Maybe a few were future Marines. Still, they were too young to be of any social or romantic interest, and given my mediocre skateboarding skills, they paid me no attention.

Then a brunette about my age, clad in blue T-shirt and green hip-huggers, skated up, complaining of a chill in the air. She was filming an all-girl skate documentary, she said, jerking her head towards a guy behind her holding a video camera. I, in bulky kneepads and the same wrist guards I'd owned since seventh grade, remained on the sidelines of the ramp. When I finally dropped in, I tried to turn, lost my balance, and had to bail. I knee-slid down the ramp and scrambled up to the same side as the blue-shirted girl. She cracked to the blond, "looks like we have the next child prodigy over here," slyly pointing to me. Then she dropped into the ramp, flew through the air, and performed a fifty-fifty grind on the coping, a cigarette dangling between two ivory fingers.

Suddenly I was back in middle school, and she'd morphed into a punk version of the popular girls who'd cast me out. I'd seen this at Officer Candidates School, too—women outnumbered by men, putting each other down. I didn't yet have the inkling that maybe Marla could have felt this way about my sharing our comrades' perspective in Iraq.

I said nothing and moved to a four-foot-tall miniramp, more crowded but easier to navigate. The male skaters there ignored me; the only girl there, closer to me in ability, had come with her boyfriend. She seemed friendly, but I didn't engage her. Once bitten, twice shy.

The crowd thinned as the sky darkened; we all fell hard as seaside fog descended on wood and metal. I rubbed my skinned elbow and kept going. As the hurt dissipated from my also-bruised ego, it occurred to me that maybe I shouldn't feel too bad about the blue-shirted girl's earlier barb; guys heckled each other way worse. Skaters left as the streetlights came on; the cameraman kept filming. When the girl in blue finished her run on the ramp, I tapped her on the calf with my board.

"Good luck with your documentary," I said.

She looked me in the eye, and with a genuine smile said, "thank you."

Awkwardly deflecting unexpected kindness, I said, "And for the record, I've never been cool in my life, so I'm not gonna start now."

Her eyes wide and serious, she replied, "Why not?"

I chuckled, embarrassed and tongue-tied, and skated away as her videographer replayed her footage.

As I hopped off the curb and skated down the street to my car, I mulled it over. Why not? There was no good reason.

Once or twice on those skate park nights, I took Buster and let him pull me. The wheel-roar on pavement egged him on, and he ran faster. His leash slackened as my skateboard sped up. Maybe, then, it felt to him as if he were free.

• • •

At Maintenance Battalion I soon latched onto a crew of other company-grade officers; nearly all of them had deployed, and together we commiserated about office-bound life. I wrote parodies of our dry manuals to make them laugh. At an Anaheim Angels baseball game, a female captain friend and I dove under our seats the first time the stadium shot firecrackers to mark a home run. We rose sheepishly, but steeled ourselves at each subsequent crack of the bat.

I hid as best I could the survivor guilt that swelled anytime I sat in traffic. Why had the troops from my nightmares died, and not I, who'd compromised my moral high ground? How could I help Mullins? Grief gathered and dissipated; like San Diego's layered clouds, it would burn off for an afternoon but return the next morning. Though my colleagues treated me kindly, and probably would have listened, I didn't bring up Mullins around them, nor did I confide in them about Jack—or any of my emotions, save the "safe" ones involving anger or snarky hilarity. The colleague with whom I'd attended the baseball game called me, not unkindly, "a very hard person to read." Looking back, I'd agree with her. I feared she'd think less of me if I told her anything.

Still, these friends provided more comfort than they knew. Saturday mornings I stowed my glasses in my car, zipped the car key into my shorts, and padded barefoot to the surf shop to join them. We'd stumble out onto the beach, heavy foam rental boards balanced on our heads. My limbs hung too short to do the cool surfer-chick thing of slinging the board under one arm. When the wind blew, our boards became giant sails.

Surfing took innate balance and control, yes, but you had

no control over the frequency or height of waves washing over you. You rode them only as best you could. I'd grown used to planning and prepping, to-do lists and regimented schedules. I'd made an academic pursuit of everything I'd ever tried. If I could just learn things in digestible bites and train with steady rubrics, I thought I'd succeed. Surfing, though, brought blindness and disarray. I paddled lopsided. Kelp wrapped around my arms. I pissed my wetsuit, like most of us did, but no one admitted to.

My friends surrounded me, bobbing stomach-down on their boards, craning their necks to spot likely waves. It didn't matter whether or not I looked; without my glasses, the sea and sky melded into one gray-blue blob. I whipped my head around, taking cues from my blurry comrades. I started paddling when everyone else did.

I often fell behind on waves, not paddling fast or strong enough. I paddled even when I didn't have to, thinking all that effort would make me a better surfer. When a steel-gray wall rose behind me, I cleaved to my board and hoped I didn't die. When the sea's force flung me at just the right moment, the wave-curl sucked back my board, and I had no choice but to catch it. But what then, when the weight of the entire ocean lapped at me? I jumped off. Success was more terrifying than failure. I bailed over and over again. Sometimes, I leaned too far forward, and the board nosedived into the water. I flew ass-over-teakettle and flipped underwater, confused until lightening bubbles guided me airward. Everyone else looked like they were having fun, but I couldn't quite catch my balance. I tried analyzing my friends' moves. It was exhausting. After ten minutes I just wanted to take my tired bones to brunch.

But the only thing that would make me a better surfer was practice. No amount of book-study or dry-land drills would build my muscle memory. Only getting out into the waves.

Eventually we had twenty minutes left until it was time to walk up the cliff to return the boards. I wanted to let the sea push me back to the sand, stumble onto the beach, hang my head down, and empty my sinuses. I picked my way through the breaking surf. *Careful*, I thought, stumbling. I then looked at my watch again. I could spend a few minutes drying out, or . . . fuck it. I could do anything for twenty minutes. I grabbed the stiff band of webbing where the leash met the board. I walked backwards through the waves, glancing over my left shoulder, daring them to beat me again. One hit me full-on in the ribs, knocking the wind out, as if to say, "You want this, kiddo? Here ya go." When I was far enough toward the break, I lay on my stomach and paddled out, taking a few waves to the face. Better surfers shredded thirty yards away.

I watched my friends for a likely crest, then paddled hard toward shore. When the wave hit, I strained mightily to stand, but only made it up to my butt. I rode sitting halfway to the beach, let out a yell, and fell off. The sea may have beaten me, but I knew no matter how many times I somersaulted underwater, I'd end up facing skyward in the surf.

• • •

With less than a year left on my Marine Corps contract, I craved control over my next career step. I was tired of obeying the rules governing everything from haircuts to dating. I wanted to have a stable cohort of friends, not watch them deploy just as I got to know them. I also wanted to move someplace where none of my colleagues had a chance of finding out about Jack.

I applied to several graduate schools on the East Coast, which still felt like home, though my undergrad experiments in particle physics seemed impractical after deployment. Materials science felt much more solid: everything from polymers to batteries to techniques for building microprocessors. I spent autumn evenings in an Encinitas coffee shop, studying for the GRE and composing admissions essays amid scents of patchouli and cardamom. I described the angel I'd watched Jack process and speculated how stronger armor materials could protect people. Though part of it felt like shamelessly trotting out death and destruction, it was the first honest writing I'd shown anyone about Iraq.

I tried to hit on guys who shared my coffee-shop tables—never successfully. One night, open mic started at my favorite haunt, and a fine-haired surfer cradled his guitar. The music grew loud and distracting; I couldn't make out the equations in my workbook. I listened for a minute, anxiety building. The crowd swelled; the espresso machine blasted. I had to get out of there. I shoved my books into a backpack and took one last look at the singer as I left. Nothing would stand in the way of my escape.

By that spring, Columbia had accepted me for a PhD program in materials science. When I visited, the program's administrator offered me the locations of cafes and sunny benches, and left me alone. For this I felt grateful. If I was going to spend five years getting a degree, I wanted to be somewhere I could hide.

My enthusiastic roommates threw me a getting-out-of-the-Marine-Corps party on Cinco de Mayo. I filled the piñata with candy and condoms. Nell posted good-luck signs around the house: Fozzie Bear with the caption, "I can't believe you're leaving us, bitch!" and Buster with a speech bubble: "don't forget to take me with you!" As I chomped chips and guac, I felt grateful for my friends.

With Camp Pendleton in the rearview that summer, I visited North Carolina; Marla was stationed on an East Coast base.

TWENTY

Gone to Carolina

Redeployment Day plus Twenty-One Months

Marla met me in Wilmington. We hadn't seen each other in the six months since she'd moved. In the interim, I'd gotten contact lenses, grown my hair to my shoulders, and bought tighter T-shirts, like the pink one I wore now. I'd dropped a few pounds from daily long runs and lifting boxes while moving cross-country. The weed-whacking, brush-clearing week I'd just spent on my uncle's nearby farmstead had browned my arms and legs. And as long as I wasn't striding head-forward down the street or splaying my legs in a seated slouch, I could pass for feminine. Marla looked the same as ever, slender and athletic in slim-fit jeans and red ponytail.

We walked Wilmington's quaint downtown, pausing to sit on an oak-slatted bench. Our conversation circled back to Iraq. It always did.

"Today's Jack's birthday," I said. In my mind, I counted two years since I'd visited his bunker. A year since that stupid email.

At the drop of his name, Marla reminisced about the mortuary affairs duties they'd performed together. Because she'd assisted him with the work, she carried more baggage than I ever would—vivid nightmares and intrusive thoughts of guts and blood and distended faces. Since coming home, I'd sometimes felt guilty and unworthy for not having assisted in mortuary affairs, though in Iraq I hadn't cared.

"That MA stuff was so fucked up," she said.

"Uh-huh," I mumbled. I had my own memories of that bunker—of the entire deployment. At least I no longer jumped quite as much at loud noises.

"I never told you this," she said, "but Jack and I had a little thing going on at the beginning of the deployment."

I froze. "What?"

"He hit on me," she said.

Her? First?

"Wait," I blurted, "he totally hit on me, too! I had a thing going on with him, too!"

We blinked at each other. Opened our mouths, gulped only air. And started laughing.

"That. Rat. Fucking. Bastard." I said.

She said in a rush, "I thought you were the good one! That you were this perfect little lieutenant, that you had the best deployment ever, and there was something wrong with me!"

"Nope. I was totally fucked up," I said. "Mother. Fucker. When was it?"

"At the beginning. Then things with 'Major Glory' happened quickly."

"Think was there overlap between you and me?"

"Maybe," Marla said.

I blew out a sharp breath. "Fucking. Bastard." I said. "I wanna punch him in the face."

I wasn't special; all along, I'd been Jack's second choice. No matter how much he'd said he loved me, or how I'd kept up appearances with my good-lieutenant act, Marla's graceful gait and demure smile had outdone me before I ever knew I had a chance. But now, I didn't blame her; I blamed Jack—and myself, for being so dumb.

We walked to an empty restaurant, climbed creaky stairs, and sipped beers on a wrought-iron balcony. We pieced together chronology and details, high-fived each other at the sick irony of it all. Spilt beer dripped through the wired-aluminum table. "So fucked up," I said, as we pecked at arugula salads. Marla stared off to the side, shook her head, murmured agreement.

• • •

Driving back north with Buster in the backseat, I thought I'd flip Quantico, where Jack was still stationed, a single-fingered salute. I'd unveil digital revenge as soon as I hit Wi-Fi range—would register the domain name *jacktempleisalyingsackofshit. blogspot.com*—maybe even at one of those highway service plazas with free Wi-Fi. Within a few hours, empty coffee cups littered my car; high on caffeine, I got angrier. Maybe I wouldn't bypass Quantico after all. Maybe I'd march into Jack's cubicle; he worked in a building nicknamed the "Death Star." I'd scream in front of everyone how I hoped Sebastian realized what an asshole his old man was. Then I wanted to deck him—maybe even give him a black eye—and storm out. On I ranted as I wove through tiny Carolina towns, shouting, "Mother FUCKER!" over the steering wheel.

Then as I hit 64 West, a Christian rock song hummed on the radio. Many New Yorkers wouldn't admit this, but I sometimes listened to Christian rock on long car rides, soothed by major chords and wholesome lyrics.

The singer belted something about not being judgmental. About forgiveness. And, still caffeinated, I got a much bolder idea. I could confront Jack and punch him. Or I could forgive him. Face-to-face.

Suddenly I needed to make it to Quantico before four thirty, close of business.

I'd had Jack's work phone number memorized for months, though I'd never called it. When I dialed, he answered.

I hung up.

I hadn't expected him to *actually be at his desk.*

I took a deep breath and hit redial, remembering how he'd jokingly answered my calls on TQ.

"What're you wearing?" I said.

He knew it was me.

When I pulled into the Death Star's parking lot, I spotted his stilted gait at fifty yards. The air felt liquid. Aside from wearing woodland camouflage, he looked the same. We didn't touch as we greeted each other. We walked Buster into the woods, down a gravelly trail. I sweated through my T-shirt. A lone runner, gray-haired and crew-cut, huffed past us. No one else knew we were out there. I waited until the runner had passed. Then I dropped the leash and threw gravel into the woods, stone by stone, as hard as I could. I hadn't yet told Jack why I'd come. Now I was only surprised I hadn't found out earlier.

I sputtered something like *how does it feel to have no integrity* peppered with *what the fuck* and *motherfucker* and *MARLA?*

He stood still and sighed.

"I didn't think it was worth mentioning," he said, patient, as if with a child. "Marla and I had what we had, and you and I had what we had," he said. "I wanted to keep that separate and private."

I fumed more *what-the-fucks* and *did you just go for me because you couldn't have her?*

"When I first met you, I thought you were cute," he said. "Then I got to talk with you. You were amazing."

I only half-believed him. I asked how many others there were, how stupid I'd been.

"No," he said. "T, there was no one else."

I threw more gravel and let Buster off-leash.

"Whatever," I said. "I really came here to punch you in the face."

"If that's all you want, you can hit me," Jack said.

I eyed him, wary but excited.

"If you need to break my nose to make you feel better, go ahead and do it," he said.

I Velcroed my MIT ring into my shorts' mesh pocket. Jack stood facing me, angled sixty degrees to the side.

When I said, "Lean down a little," he obliged.

I wound my hips back, just as we'd trained. He flinched. Fist met flesh. I'd gotten him near his ear, not exactly what I wanted, but a solid hit.

He winced and stepped back. His ear must have been ringing. Blinking, shaking it off, he said, "You pivoted your heel really well."

I hucked a last gravel chunk into the woods. We sat down on fallen branches by a small creek. Buster waded in and lapped cool water.

"Were you lying when you said you loved me?" I said.

"No," he said. "No."

"Do you know what it's like to spend two years hating yourself?" I said.

"I know how that feels," he said. "My life is shit."

He'd gotten into a bar fight a few months before. A guy had said something bad about the Marine Corps; Jack had broken his arm. I remembered him demonstrating armbars on Mullins and Sanchez; he must have whipped the guy in the same way. I pictured Jack later, contrite, flanked by lawyers.

This was real, the shit we used to warn our Marines against during Friday safety briefs. Warrant officers—especially ones in line for promotion, like Jack—could derail their careers if this happened enough.

They'd sent him to shrinks. He said it seemed like he'd seen every therapist the Marine Corps could hire. The most recent one, he said, was sort of helping.

Soon we walked back to the trailhead. It had been two hours since I'd pulled into the parking lot.

"Can we be friends now?" he asked.

"I don't know."

Now that I was free of the Corps, could this so-called friendship—or whatever it was—work? Could he, of all people, help me let go of the shame and survivor guilt I still carried? Did that punch help me forgive him? I wasn't sure.

"Can I at least email you?" he asked.

I looked up at him, at his reddened ear. Remembered "No One Left Behind" spelled out on the roof of his bunker.

"I guess so."

TWENTY-ONE

A Little Trouble in the Big Apple

New York, New York—Redeployment Day plus Two Years

Summer sweltered in New York, two years and 100 percent humidity beyond Iraq. As smoke alarms bled into sirens, I dragged my bags into an open living room—my new bedroom—in an apartment with three other roommates. Armed with a borrowed drill, I assembled a life.

I bought a door and carried it seventeen blocks, down sidewalks sprinkled with dogshit. Moved a desk upstairs piece-by-piece, pushing a granny cart in one hand, pulling a dog leash in the other. Wondered which drugs could have been smoked from the burnt Pepsi can on the stoop. Peeled supermarket stickers off pears to reveal rotting divots. Wore camouflage cutoffs to the skate park, tied Buster to its chain-link fence, and tried to fit in.

I didn't make friends in the first month. Instead, I spent nights on the floor of my room, petting Buster's velvety ears as the radiator hissed. I drank cheap wine and made phone calls to Marine officer buddies with whom I hadn't deployed. I missed the ease and camaraderie of military life. In the Corps, friends freely offered car maintenance, moving help, dinners, and dog care as part of an interpersonal barter system; people did each other so many favors that we simply lost track. I hadn't found a similar cohort in New York yet. Instead, Columbia's crime-report bulletins tuned me to the same timbre of rage I'd mentally directed towards the Iraqi laborers who'd stared at and catcalled me. I used problem sets and exams as excuses not to socialize with my new classmates.

I wandered into Central Park to study alone, briefcase bopping on my hip much as my CamelBak did years before. I still felt like the same lieutenant, only instead of contemplating the least-broken chair in the tea garden, I deliberated on the perfect bench on which to ram math and electrodynamics into my brain.

Every morning I ran, counting calories in granola bars. Buster's lunchtime jaunt added an extra hour's daily walk. I lost ten more pounds in a month, only half-meaning to. Between the stress of school and the weight loss, my periods stopped. My doctor's advice could be distilled into six words worthy of Michael Pollan: "Sit down. Chill out. Eat something."

Despite slimming down, I didn't bother buying anything flattering; women's clothing still felt too revealing. Instead I wore T-shirts from middle school and patched my ripped jeans, looping my belt tighter when a colleague pointed out my plumber's crack.

I felt far more of an affinity with other Marines than I did while on active duty, scanning city streets for goatees and low-reg haircuts and combat boots with jeans—surefire markers of men who'd just left the military. I could pick out high and tight haircuts from blocks away and knew which pilled fabric marked issued USMC gym sweats. Columbia had an organization for military veterans, but I felt too shy to make their acquaintance. People might ask questions, might assume I had been in combat. I'd feel like a fraud—guilty of staying "inside the wire" while deployed. I certainly didn't want to confess what had happened with Jack. Seven years later, I'd find solace in veterans' writing workshops—where no one, in fact, would judge me—but in grad school, I stayed far away.

In class I tripped over once-familiar concepts: identity matrices, eigenvalues. One afternoon a loud bang reverberated down the hallway, shaking our hard plastic chairs through the cinderblock. I visibly jumped. "Fuckin' flashbacks," I muttered, as our unflappable prof droned on about Brillouin zones and k-space.

I found out later that the bang was likely from a lab research-ing concussive shocks that caused traumatic brain injuries. An IED or mortar is exactly what that noise was supposed to sound like. Out of context, it sounded even more real. This did not make me feel any less of a damaged freak.

I waded into the social scene slowly. Most people in my grad-uate department were supportive of my service, but not quite all. Our young department secretary, Sylvie, was new at her job. She came to the grad student happy hour one Friday after I sat down, Buster at my side. She ordered her vodka neat; I drank Diet Coke.

On Sylvie's second drink, the subject of military service came up, though I don't recall how she knew I'd been in. Perhaps she really wanted to hear from George, the handsome, triathlete air force veteran next to me. The rest of the guys at the table were young American students; at least two were sons of veterans.

"I'm a pacifist," Sylvie said. "I think war's stupid." She swirled her vodka.

Fine, whatever, I thought, *it takes all kinds.* I could sure make a case for war being stupid.

"War's wrong," she said. "I would *never* go to war."

Again—fine. Never mind that going wasn't exactly my choice—nor was this most recent war the choice of many Amer-icans, either. George shrugged and was about to speak.

"Why would you even *join* the military?" she said, looking directly at me, tossing her head. "I would *never* choose to be in the military."

It wasn't what she said, which was mild enough. It was her snotty tone, its judgment, and its direction specifically at me. Never mind that George and I had both served; at least we'd come home safe. But my friends were still deploying. Friends-of-friends and former colleagues had died. Sylvie's dismissal implied all of this was vulgar, base, and above all, due to *our* poor personal choices as veterans. Discussing war, to her, was as if someone in that faux-Irish pub had asked her to hitch up her pretty skirt and pick up dogshit with her manicured hands. Maybe provoking controversy was her way of trying to look cool. Or maybe she felt competitive and put me down because I was the only other woman at the table.

Anger rose in my throat, and I stood. Buster got up, too, rattling his chain leash. I felt wrath at the slightest provocation in those days, but still thought it would look bad to get kicked out of grad school for punching the department secretary.

"You better be glad that I am who I am, and my friends and I do what we do, so you have the freedom to say what you say," I said loudly, leaning forward and pointing an index finger. Rage and shame burned up my chest. Was I now that stereotypical angry veteran?

Sylvie's smile froze into an awkward mask. She tried to backpedal, said something about "healthy debate."

George raised a hand and said something reasonable while I glared at Sylvie. She shut up and sipped her vodka. I left soon after.

Friends materialized in the coming weeks; not all had been at the pub, but they'd heard the story and supported me. Kevin was a married army infantry major studying physics in order to teach at West Point. He took a shine to Buster. Though I didn't speak of Iraq, and he mentioned little of his own deployments, we kept each other awake through partial differential equations and hashed out exam practice problems together. Neil was a smartass native New Yorker fresh out of undergrad. We took the same nanotechnology class, where we learned the engineering and chemistry behind small-scale devices. I hoped to do research with the professor, who one morning surprised us with a breakfast of doughnut holes. Neil turned to me and whispered, "Wanna have a doughnut-eating contest?"

"No, we cannot have a doughnut-eating contest," I said, smiling at his familiar rambunctiousness. He reminded me of my Marines.

Still, I confided in none of these friends about my recurring nightmares. I had more in New York than I ever did in California: gruesome bodies, legs and hands and chewed-up torsos. In one I debated whether to take Buster with me into a firefight, unsure of what I'd feed him, unable to simultaneously grip a dog leash and an M16. On bad nights, I lay awake, echoing thoughts I'd learn years later were all too common among veterans.

I should have stayed in the Corps, should have deployed again, should have gone back to Iraq, should have died there. There was only ever one body I watched them process. I didn't do anything.

There was a Mortuary Affairs billet that came available just before I left, I thought. *I should have taken it—should have done Jack's job better than him. I could have righted my mistakes.*

I secretly liked my revved-up self-flagellation; it made me feel more human—or at least made me feel *something*. It reminded me the war had been real; even adopting a negative identity meant I still possessed an identity. And it felt familiar—Marine Corps training, in glorifying selfless sacrifice, moral perfection, and personal responsibility, only encouraged this particular brand of rumination.

With a few months' distance from the head-punching incident in Quantico, I thought Jack could help me transition out of the Marine Corps, or at least convince me that I was moving forward honorably with my life. Then I wouldn't have to risk the vulnerability of venturing out with new friends. He'd understand the anger that whelmed me, because he'd felt it, too. Maybe he'd talk to me with the compassion and understanding I craved but couldn't muster for myself. *He would have to*, I thought. Few others knew what we'd experienced in Iraq. And his platoon left no one behind.

Most nights I stayed disciplined. But one Sunday afternoon in my first semester, the taste of a neighborhood cafe's shawarma cracked me open. I emailed him about sweet-spicy chicken and patio chairs, and he gave me his new phone number.

The next time I had a bad night, I called him. Supine on my room's wooden floor, I pressed the phone to my ear. "I keep seeing bodies in my dreams," I told him as Buster settled next to me.

Jack said, "Everyone comes back with something. You'd be weird if you *didn't* have those dreams." His voice soothed me, but I knew if I kept phoning, I'd have trouble breaking the habit. To avoid the potential indignity of unreturned calls, I made no more. Jack couldn't save me from my nightmares, and I couldn't save him. It felt familiar: not-calling, not-emailing, congratulating myself on each consecutive week of noncontact. Every night I made the choice not to call, I recommitted to my new, separate path.

• • •

Over Christmas break I would see Joe Gregory, the high-school crush who had told me of Ms. Hopper's unusual marriage. He'd approached me online, had a baby son, and was in the midst of an amicable divorce. I wondered if I emitted some pheromone that drew guys estranged from their wives, and I felt slightly guarded as he and I made plans to catch up in Maryland.

Though I stayed at my mom's house for the holidays, I told her nothing of Joe, save that he was a friend from high school. I certainly didn't call the evening a date, though I'd blow-dried my hair and put on a rare going-out outfit: a merino wool turtleneck and slim black pants that highlighted the weight I'd lost. The way I still saw it, my mom had fucked up our lives when she'd married our stepdad; she didn't get a say in my relationships.

Joe picked me up on my mother's doorstep a few nights before Christmas, wearing far fewer earrings than the several-per-ear he'd worn in high school. Other than that, he looked mostly the same: wavy brown hair, a matching goatee. He even had on the same leather jacket as the last time I'd seen him, when I'd been fifteen and he'd been eighteen. And perhaps my olfactory memory had manufactured it, but I could have sworn he still wore the same Stetson cologne.

At the pub, we talked nose-to-nose over beers and artichoke dip. He knew I'd served in the military, but I told him no details about Iraq, maintaining the image of a well-adjusted grad student. Soon he pulled a crinkled sheet of loose-leaf from his jacket. It was a letter I'd written him after my freshman year of high school, thanking him for paying attention to me, for listening to the oldies station while we painted sets for stage crew, for understanding about my stepfather. Joe had had a tough stepdad, too. Back when he'd first gotten the letter, he said, it had made him cry. As he and his ex-wife were splitting up their belongings, he'd found it again.

I traced my teenage scribble on the now-translucent paper. Joe said he'd realized that it was his stepfather who'd driven him to hockey practice, who'd supported him in choosing an artistic college major. He'd made peace with the man, and with his real father, too.

He asked me how my parents were. I said they were okay, sort of. They still pissed me off, but at least I didn't have to live there anymore or tell them anything about my life.

As it grew late, he leaned in closer and told me something more salacious: when he was a senior, he said, he'd had sex with a pretty, twenty-three-year-old teacher at our school. I spluttered beer through my nose. "No way!"

"Yes way!"

He leaned over his drink, eyes glinting. I smiled, encouraging him. Though he dropped me home that night with nothing more than a hug, by early spring, he called me every evening. I thought he was joking when he lobbed a few cheesy pickup lines my way.

Then he blew off a guys' poker weekend to visit my crowded apartment. Looking back, I should have realized these were signals of interest, but I didn't, or wouldn't, believe them. He hadn't found me attractive at fourteen, and I couldn't conceive of us both changing in the intervening dozen years. I had neither cleaned the bathroom nor put on flattering clothes by the time his car pulled up.

We sat on the floor of my room and played Spit and Egyptian Rat Screw, the same card games we'd played in high school. Feeling comfortably nostalgic for those pre-Marine Corps days, I also replayed my teenage awkwardness. I didn't make lingering eye contact, nor did I let my limbs linger suggestively near his. It wouldn't have gone further unless he'd said something romantic or wrapped me up in a kiss. I'd grown used to the lightning pace of military courtship; without rocket attacks and high testosterone to speed attraction, relationship-building in the civilian world seemed mellower, more time-dilated.

So I studiously avoided thinking about why Joe might leave his friends at a casino and drive three hours just to play cards and eat Indian food with me. When he cried, "Spit!" and clapped his hand over mine, his goatee split into a grin, but I didn't make any moves. He picked up on my shy hesitation and didn't push it. He slept on an air mattress in my room, pale belly peeking from under a faded T-shirt. We parted in the morning after egg-and-bacon sandwiches, coffee for me, Red Bull for him.

But even if Joe had come on to me more strongly, I don't think I would have embraced another relationship with a half-divorced father. The details of Joe's separation remained fuzzy, and I didn't relish the prospect of again competing with a child for a man's attention. I couldn't admit it then, but I'll admit it now—I felt relieved when he drove away.

TWENTY-TWO

Get By with a Little Help

New York—Redeployment Day plus Three and a Half Years

Over the next year, I entered a vortex of lab research, paper writing, and conferences, pausing only for harried dog walks and meals of grilled cheese. Without Marine Corps rules to hold me back or prop me up, nonstop work numbed my feelings and lent a virtuous sheen to my frantic activity. Under chemical hoods, I tinkered with tweezers and dunked glass slides into acetone and isopropanol. I learned to vaporize metal into patterns and shoot lasers at fluorescent-dyed DNA, donning woven bonnets, clean room bunny suits, and nitrile gloves identical to the ones that had lined the shelves in Jack's bunker. I passed qualifying exams and oral exams and my thesis proposal.

I felt lonely, but meeting new people was sharper agony.

I still smelled Iraq during the change of seasons, air-conditioning and hardboiled egg yolk, roasted dust in the SYSCON on dry evenings. Rosewater cologne in a subway car transported me to Kuwaiti cribbage games. Spoonfuls of green tea fro-yo evoked my tea-studded soap in the shower trailer. Blazing sun brought me back to the fiber lay. Outkast's "Hey Ya" blasted down the block, beating SYSCON Dance Party loud in my head. Every few months, I'd succumb to clickbait news from the war. Mullins was eventually acquitted. Sometimes Sanchez phoned me or sent a Facebook message. Afterward,

I'd look at old digital photos from our deployment. I peered at Jack's smooth thirty-six-year-old face, the olive cheeks that had hollowed and paled with each passing month, the hairline that had kept receding. At those moments I'd wonder how he looked, if his fillings still showed when he laughed, if his tattoos had faded.

Then I'd lift my hands from the keyboard, knowing I needed to concentrate on making friends in Manhattan.

Every day in lab I shoved myself in front of people who soon became familiar. When friends insisted on pulling me out of my workaholic mode, I found myself more receptive than when Marla had invited me out with pilots, or when Clive had wanted to share beers. I still dragged Buster to bars and parties: an easy icebreaker, but also an excuse to leave early if I needed to. Eventually I felt comfortable enough to socialize without ducking away.

As my Marine Corps comrades settled down with longtime boyfriends and girlfriends, I felt like a lost sock, the only person on the planet left unpaired. Crushes came and went; none liked me back. The men I met at bars and at sporting events seemed to want women who acted more feminine than I did. Not a woman who could be attractive in old jeans and no makeup, or one who skateboarded and got knocked down in clumsy hockey. Or perhaps it was the whiff of desperation that spooked them. I never flirted, only confessed my attraction awkwardly and too late. I compared myself to younger women, their lipsticked smiles and clip-clopping heels subtle torture for me in my sneakers.

Slowly I worked on my appearance: a flowery shirt from Old Navy, a set of dangly earrings, a clip to tame my wild mane into a bun. Finally I dressed up for the weekly grad student happy hour. I carried a backpack-type purse and tried not to think of myself as a *girl*—the word spat out like Skoal in a dip cup—for carrying a bag. The night ended with bar songs.

In our third semester of grad school, Kevin and his wife divorced, and he unburdened himself on long dog walks. I still hadn't spoken much of my service with him, but if I'd learned

nothing else from the Marines, it was how to talk with divorcing men. Knowing his trials gave me the courage to be vulnerable, too. One evening in Central Park, after I'd chased Buster
away from a forgotten bagel, I admitted that I was profoundly
unhappy, and revealed what had happened with Jack in Iraq. It
was the most I'd said on the subject since coming home.

"Maybe you should talk to someone," Kevin said.

It seemed everyone in New York had a therapist, but I still felt
like a failure sitting in a chair for my first appointment. I told my
shrink I felt destroyed. I tried to unravel how it all happened in
the first place, narrated my broken childhood, the pain-desire-
guilt spiral that wouldn't disappear. I rarely mentioned counseling to my friends. *No one must know this*, I thought. *They can't
find out I'm not normal.* I continued seeing the shrink, quietly,
for six months. Talking helped.

Also helpful were the girlfriends of guys in my graduate
department, who plied me with questions and hugs and cookies and ceviche. Who invited me camping and assembled homemade trail mix. Who ensured I scored invites to clothing swaps,
beer-pong bars, and parties at their boyfriends' apartments,
where everyone taped malt liquor bottles to their hands while
wearing wigs. Who loved Buster and bought him treats and
walked him when I went out of town for yet another wedding
of old Marine friends. Who didn't know what had happened in
Iraq. They just knew that I could cook a mean marinara sauce
and would help schlep a piano keyboard from Brooklyn to Har-
lem in my Toyota. After a few months, I trusted them like sisters, their boyfriends like brothers.

Marla even came up one weekend for a charity 5K run. Five
of us ran: three girlfriends from grad school, her, and me. We
took the subway to Roosevelt Island, where a brand-new Starbucks poked out from half-finished condos. Marla and I finally
looked similar—she in running tights and polar fleece, me in a
small, bright-blue sweatshirt and track pants. We wore our hair
swept back in ponytails against the wind. We jogged along the

asphalt pathways, past brick buildings stenciled like cellblocks. Construction plastic flapped in strong winds. At the end, we passed a smorgasbord of goodie bags containing lotions and lip balm. I took a bag unselfconsciously, eyeing the moisturizer. The postrace cocoa warmed us, and we settled down for coffee at the communal table of an uptown pastry chain. We five women split baskets of bread smeared with Nutella and jam. We gossiped about people we knew, ordered lunch, and traded stories about men. By the time the check came, I felt sleepy, well fed, and cared for. I didn't feel nerdy or out of place, as I had with my middle-school classmates or California roommates. Nor did I feel the need to judge Marla's femininity; I was "one of the girls" now, too. For once, I didn't feel like our deployment secrets were the centerpiece of our friendship.

And though my old lieutenant self would have been mortified, I asked my girlfriends to help me dress better. Maya, Lori, and Abby took me to places I felt unqualified to enter: Forever 21. Banana Republic. Express. They dressed me in a skirt and tight sweater, practice for my ten-year high school reunion. Unless softball eye-black and camouflage face paint counted, I had never before smeared on my own makeup. Lori gifted me a palette of eyeshadow. Maya held my chin, brushed shadow on my lids, and showed me how to blend different colors: light purple first, then dark brown from the inside corner. These complemented the green flecks in my eyes, she explained. She and Lori wielded the hair dryer, burning my ears while rolling a round brush through my thin locks. I felt silly just sitting there, but the girls were gentle and smiley. I had never thought to ask for this before. I could get used to playing dress-up, I thought, this praise for feminine displays instead of assuming everyone would roll their eyes at me. My friends didn't know it, but they were pasting me together.

TWENTY-THREE

Crash

Joe Gregory was doing well during my third summer of grad school. In the two years since I'd seen him in New York, he'd started a nonprofit, had found new love, and was planning to marry again. His son was three years old.

Joe took his last motorcycle ride on a July afternoon in Maryland. The crash killed him instantly. The day after it happened, I drove south for the memorial.

In Maryland I met Joe's ex-wife, the mother of their boy. She remembered stories about me from high school and the letter I'd written him. On a card I scrawled as many memories of him as I could remember: his shredded jeans and backwards baseball cap, the Marlboro packs strewn on the floor of his car, how he'd played the baseline to Green Day's "Longview" on electric bass.

Joe was my first friend to die. I realized how colossally lucky I'd been during the war. Everyone I knew had made it home.

Driving back north after the memorial service, I rolled up my car windows against the wind. It was just past eleven, the same time Jack and I used to play chess in the tea garden. I thought about his hitting on Marla, his lies of omission, his scarcity. In the face of mortality, none of it mattered. I still cared for him, wherever he was, and I didn't want him to die without knowing it. Though we hadn't spoken in two and a half years, I wondered if he still thought about me.

On the Jersey Turnpike, I called 411, asked for Jack's home phone number, and let them patch me through. His wife answered.

I took a deep breath and asked for Jack. He wasn't home.

I left her my name and number; she said she would give him the message. Her voice registered neither recognition nor suspicion. I felt numb when the phone clicked off.

Twenty minutes later, it rang. "You're the love of my life, T," Jack said.

We spent the next two hours on the phone while I drove. He lived on a houseboat near Norfolk during the week and drove north to a DC suburb on weekends. He was still married, and was about to retire from the Corps. Sebastian was thirteen. In the five years since TQ, Jack had been through a dozen shrinks and nearly as many meds. In his sleep, he still saw dead Marines.

"I think about you all the time," he said. "I think about the ball a lot."

His bedtime ritual was Ambien and scotch. He warned me that he'd sound fuzzy just before he hung up. Hopped up on emotion from the memorial service, I told him I didn't want him to die without knowing that I had loved him.

"I love you, too," he said, slipping towards unconsciousness.

TWENTY-FOUR

No One Left Behind

In the following weeks, we talked every couple of nights. On the eve of my birthday, I stood in the kitchen baking cookies. My cell phone rang. I ungloved my hand from the burnt mitt, flipped open my phone. It was Jack.

"Hey," he said, "I'm outside."

"No, you're not," I said, except I'd heard an echo through the open window.

"I'm here a day early. Thought I'd surprise you, help you celebrate your birthday," he said.

I left the cookie sheet on the counter, smoothed my hair, ran downstairs, sock-slid on the tiled lobby floor, flung open the door, and jumped into his arms. I knocked off his silly porkpie hat, and he dropped a wooden cane. A green T-shirt swayed on his six-foot-two frame. He'd been driving for six hours.

When I'd mentioned the party and rattled off my address a few weeks before, I hadn't believed he would come.

Upstairs, he put down his backpack in my living room. He was balder, thicker than I remembered.

We sat on my sagging loveseat; it dipped us shoulder-to-shoulder. I shifted slightly to face him. A chocolate chip stained my favorite shirt; I didn't care.

Resting his cane along the couch, he explained he couldn't walk more than a few blocks unassisted. He'd fallen off a seven-ton back in Iraq. I didn't remember the accident; maybe it had

happened after I'd left, when their convoy had been hit by an
IED. That, I remembered. Jack had had vertebra surgery and
was in the process of being granted a medical retirement. Still,
he seemed largely the same; when he smiled, his dimples puckered into the shape I remembered so well.

I told him about school, about my nanotech research, about
how good it was to see him.

We reminisced about his old Marines. Sanchez was in college, majoring in sociology. Judging from his Facebook posts,
he hadn't lost his sense of humor: "I know I'm signed up for
classes but totally forgot what I signed up for," he wrote. "I think
that is how I joined the Marine Corps . . ."

Hoss, on the other hand, had taken a job digging graves at a
VA cemetery in Colorado, which exacerbated his PTSD. "I have
to keep him from killing himself every couple of weeks," Jack
said. I'd nearly forgotten about his ethos of care; he took personal
credit for keeping his former troops alive, not seeming to realize that not all of their lives depended directly upon him now.

We spoke of the injured Iraqi pigeon he'd adopted, an esca-
pade neither of us had talked about in five years. Gray-and-
white "Fred" had hopped one-legged on Jack's fake-linoleum
floor, wearing a homemade splint. By way of a nest, Jack had
assembled a fluff of shredded paper towels and an old T-shirt
atop his plywood bookshelf. After a couple weeks' recupera-
tion, Jack had set a healed Fred free. In those days he'd cared
for me, too, offering solace when I needed it but couldn't ask.
Now, half a decade later, I'd grown used to caring for myself.

Around 2 a.m. we grew too tired to talk anymore. I let Jack
hug me good night in my bedroom. Suddenly I stood back in
his shadowed bunker, nosing the space where I knew a jiu-jitsu
tattoo still marked his chest. I knew how the hair on his belly
would crackle against his shirt, and how his left ribs thickened
into a bony knot I'd kneaded five years before. In Iraq, his love
handles had shrunk day by day as he'd stopped eating meat or
anything resembling human flesh.

Now his heft had returned, and he stood unsteadily. I couldn't resist tickling those ribs just a little. He stumbled forward, and we wrestled; he planted his heel behind mine, martial-arts style, and swept me to the floor, covering me like a turtle shell. I remembered resting on his poncho liner, cradled in the crook of his elbow after we'd grappled too long on his floor. In Iraq, secrecy had been paramount; if we'd been caught together, we would have faced disciplinary action. Here and now we could do what we wanted, and yet I promised myself I wouldn't share a bed with him. That could go nowhere good—at least not unless I got some answers. I turned my head away. "I'm not going back to TQ," I whispered. He let me wriggle out from his hold.

We stood, and he put a meaty paw on my loft bed frame. His eyes flicked upward. It swayed slightly: a deathtrap suitable only for holding my hundred and twenty pounds.

"No way," I said, grateful for my loft's flawed bolts. "We have an air mattress somewhere."

"Do you want me to sleep in the living room instead?" he asked. I thought of his six-foot-two frame on our rickety loveseat, a spinal disaster.

"No, it's okay, you can stay in my room. But definitely on the air mattress," I said.

The velvet-topped plastic groaned as we inflated it. Then he opened a zip-up pill case: Depakote for tremors. Painkillers. Sleep aids that made Ambien look like Skittles. Each bottle had its own pouch. "Good night, beautiful," he slurred, slipping into unconsciousness. "Good night, Jack," I replied, marveling that this man—after five long years—was finally staying the night. Adrenaline fluttered me awake every couple of hours.

Late the next morning, my birthday, our stomachs rumbled. "There's a place that sells shawarma nearby," I said. "Amir's. We'll go for lunch." Their pita was our closest contender for Iraqi fare.

Jack limped down the sidewalk; my former sparring partner now used a cane. When he took my hand, I felt shy; his gentle grip hinted at withered romance. Instead of crunching gravel under sandy boots, we padded slowly in sneakered feet past students like me. After a minute I let his hand go.

Half a block later, we ran into a colleague of mine, a postdoctoral researcher in a collaborating group. As we greeted each other, he nodded to Jack, slightly deferential, as if Jack was my uncle. I turned quickly toward the restaurant, so as not to have to explain. By the time we reached Amir's, Jack's legs needed a break.

I ordered us two chicken shawarmas. Jack paid. As the smell of roast meat wafted our way, I remembered the tea garden's drumbeat of wailing music, pressed layers of bread and chicken, pools of grease that collected under our plates. The teenage waiter had always brought us a tray with two glass teacups, a sugar cube beside each. Jack had left a dollar each time.

Then the staff had trucked to Fallujah, ten miles away, on a supply run. The "supplier" was a ruse; instead, terrorists kidnapped the waiters, gouged out their eyes, cut off their tongues, and murdered them. The restaurant had closed permanently, and other Iraqi workers had stopped showing up to the base.

I shook off the memory as a T-shirted man scooped hummus behind the counter. He seemed unconcerned. No chance of kidnapping while dishing our meals onto Styrofoam plates.

Our shawarmas came wrapped in thin whole-wheat pita. They were different from the doughy folds we had known in Iraq, where the baker had slapped round loaves into a clay oven. Amir's chicken, too, proved less luscious than the Iraqis' sweet, peppered chunks cut from licking flames. The baklava tasted drier than the sumptuous fly-pocked slabs we'd devoured in the desert. One thing hadn't changed, though: the flatware. We stabbed neon-pink pickles in wax paper cups with thin knives and bendy plastic forks. We took measured bites, careful not to drip sauce on our jeans. We couldn't wipe greasy fingers on dirty desert camo anymore.

To my left, a slim young mother, her baby boy, and toddler girl prepared to leave. The boy squalled as the woman wrestled him into his Snugli and fumbled for a pacifier. I looked at her with furtive longing, as I did with every mom I saw around my age. Many of my friends were married, their pregnant bellies counterpoints to my stunted adulthood. But I was twenty-nine and still single; I clawed at any possibility that I'd be a mother someday.

The young woman half-smiled and pushed an oversized stroller onto Broadway.

"Guess that'll be me in a few years. At least I hope so," I said. I fumbled my fork. "What about you?" I asked Jack. "Would you have any more kids?"

"I like little kids," he said. But he didn't say yes. He looked at his plate. Tahini ran down his stubby thumbnail. I wanted to go back to the tea garden, when our lives had been suspended over a magnetic chessboard.

I remembered the two things Jack had told me back then: that he loved me, and that he needed to be there for his son. Now Sebastian was a handful, he said, talked back to his mom, acted up at home. I'm sure it was more than typical teenage disrespect; he must have felt the unrest simmering beneath his parents' marriage.

But I could be a cool stepmom, I thought. If I reminded Jack of what we'd shared in Iraq, he might choose to be with me. I could shortcut the agony of dating in grad school and finally build a family.

Jack had advised me on how to negotiate with other officers, on how to execute a shoulder throw. Surely he could help me grow up now?

"Whatever happens," he said, staring at his massacred pita, "we'll always be friends."

His answer didn't bode well. I wanted either a real, loving relationship, or else a friend for whom romantic feelings wouldn't resurface. It didn't look like we could have either. But was our only choice to abandon each other, even after serving together at war?

• • •

Jack stuck around that night for my birthday party. I changed into a cleavage-baring dress. My apartment filled with friends. They filtered down the exposed-brick hallway and hugged me, stuffed the fridge with beer, nabbed crackers and cheddar. We tuned Pandora to hipster bands.

One labmate, Brent, all plaid shirt and Buddy Holly glasses, asked Jack how he knew me.

"We were in the war together," Jack said.

"Cool, what was your job in the military?"

"I killed people."

Brent bobbed his head to the music and sipped his beer. "Um. Right on."

Soon after, Jack touched my elbow. "I have to take a break," he said. He got jittery in crowds. "I'm just going to go for a walk around the block. Back in an hour."

My shoulders sagged with disappointment, but I only said, "Oh."

"T," he said as he left, "You have great friends. They love you."

With him gone, I found no excuse not to get roaring drunk. My Estonian labmate had gifted me her homeland's specialty liqueur. I lost track of the shots she poured. Someone found my officer's sword, and I brandished it in my low-cut dress, barely controlling the weapon in drunken drill.

A friend I'd known since seventh grade cornered me. She'd heard about Jack ever since I returned from deployment. "So?" she said, with raised eyebrows. Faking nonchalance, I said, "We'll see what happens."

At least, that's what I remember saying. In the following days, I would be told that I shouted, "For the next five years, IT'S ANYBODY'S GAME!"

I blamed the Estonian liqueur.

Jack called me to ask what flavor Gatorade I liked. I told him blue was a flavor and purple was a fruit. He hurried back with a rainbow of bottles under his arm.

As I chugged lemon-lime, his cell phone rang.

When he answered, he said, "Hang on," and thrust the handset at me. "It's Hoss," he whispered.

I took the phone.

"Hey, Hoss," I said, unsteady. We'd barely spoken in Iraq. What the hell could I tell him now?

"I'm having a hard time, ma'am," Hoss said. He didn't realize that he didn't have to call me "ma'am" anymore.

I repeated hoary platitudes out loud and in my head. "We're thinking of you, Hoss. We're here for you. I'm sorry you're having a hard time. But you've done your time. You're home now. Hang in there." *I am drunk and high on life and dammit, Jack is here, and dammit, Hoss, don't kill yourself, it's my birthday and we're back and everyone should be happy. Have a beer. Be all right. We're back. Isn't it great that we're back?*

Except we hadn't really come back. In our minds, Jack and I were still locked in his bunker. It was a headspace we entered when we felt weak and nostalgic, when a few sips of beer would lean us back in a plastic chair, awaiting the helo at 0100 'cause the trilling phone told us so. And we sat another sleep-deprived night under buzzing fluorescent lights, and my stomach ground with anxiety. We were still there. We'd never really left. I ran my fingers through the graying wisps at my temples. "Fuuuck," I said, swearing in a drawl, as Mullins would have. I knew this feeling that Hoss tried to numb with booze. I understood now, three shots of Estonian liqueur and a vat of beer in. "I totally get it, Hoss," I yelled into Jack's cell phone. "I get it. I do that, too."

Our talk lasted maybe five minutes; by the end, Hoss sounded mostly okay. Jack waved away the phone when I offered it back. I'd relieved him of his evening duty. We left no one behind. Isn't that, after all, why we'd found each other again?

After the guests left, Jack lay on the air mattress in my room, facing the ceiling. "Happy birthday, T," he said after taking his final pill. I staved off the spins with sips of Gatorade and lay down on the hardwood floor next to him. We were both exhausted.

I held his left hand in my right, but did nothing more. Not when he'd said we were only friends. Buster flopped on my other side and rattled his dog tags: my unwitting canine chaperone. When my nausea subsided, I climbed my creaking ladder to bed and slept.

Several hours later, I woke to Jack's thrashing and mumbling, his limbs spastic on the air mattress. His nightmare was a frightening sight, this six-foot man out of control. I clambered from my loft and crouched down, laid a hand on his shuddering shoulder.

"Jack, it's T, you're in New York. Jack, it's T, you're in New York," I repeated as I shook him awake. He stopped convulsing.

"Hey," I said, squinting without my glasses, "you're okay. It was a nightmare."

For the first time, I glimpsed what it must be like to be Jack's wife.

For the first time, I did not envy her.

Daybreak bled into midmorning, Advil candy coating and more Gatorade. I washed the pots and pans in which I'd baked ziti and cornbread. In the narrow kitchen, Jack edged behind me and carefully toweled them dry. We made a good team. We filled three black trash bags with empty beer bottles. They reminded me of body bags. We didn't speak of his dreams.

When he said, "I need to get going," I couldn't choke down the lump in my throat. But beneath the feeling of loss lay a seed of relief. The strong, sure Marine I once knew was gone. The new Jack would not stay. And I had spent the past five years building a life without him.

After I walked him to his car, he lifted me off my feet in a hug. I tried to steady my pulse. "Safe drive," I told him, "I love you."

"I love you, too," he said, and—one of our favorite phrases in those weeks—"it's not your fault."

"It's not yours, either," I said.

But in the end, the fault belonged to both of us.

We traded emails, phone calls, and text messages for the

next few weeks. I spun from daydreams to numbness to aching desire, demanding answers in my head. Frustrated, I texted one night, "I have trouble believing what you're telling me, old man, seeing as you're still married."

Thirty seconds later, he called. From his tone, I thought he'd just taken his meds.

"She saw it. She's pissed," he said. His wife had looked at his phone as soon as it buzzed; she'd read my message. And likely, the chain before it.

"I'm in trouble. I'll call you tomorrow," he said, and hung up.

I sank to the floor, sat cross-legged.

He didn't call.

I knew then I needed to wake up in New York, too.

TWENTY-FIVE

Reveille

I took all of the strength I'd devoted to hoping for Jack and used it for myself.

I opened up to my nucleus of New Yorkers about my relationship with the mysterious "war buddy" who'd shown up on my birthday. Over homemade pasta and too much wine, I told my girlfriends the whole saga. I worried they'd judge me and gossip. I was shocked and relieved when they didn't. Instead the guys in my graduate program sweetly offered to kick Jack's ass. I cried in public: in my apartment's tiled lobby, along Morningside Park, during early-morning jogs. I told my story to high-school friends over the phone, walking Buster late at night. I didn't care if my neighbors heard. I enrolled back in counseling. This time, my friends knew I was seeking help.

But they still wanted to know me, even knowing how fucked up I felt. They just offered hugs and compassion. This surprised me most of all.

I stopped trying to stem my sadness. I could neither save Jack nor lure him away from his family. There was no shortcut to building a life. In reaching out to my friends, I owned who I was without him. The memories and pain finally began to fade.

• • •

My mom knew I'd been stressed, but she didn't know why. A month after I'd last seen Jack, I asked her to stop by my apartment. It was rare for me to initiate contact. In the years since I'd returned from Iraq, Mom had tried to be there for me, but I'd brushed her off or fled every time deployment had come up. We'd continued our don't-ask-don't-tell policy about boyfriends, too. I hadn't consulted her on my choice of college, military service, graduate program, or living space. I strove to minimize her input into my life's trajectory.

But ever since I was a toddler, she had been able, with a single kind look, to unintentionally make me cry. It was never anything she said or did; even now, I still don't understand how it happens. But her presence had always made it all right for me to fall apart. This was, perhaps, part of the reason I'd never told her anything. I hated falling apart.

That afternoon I made us tea. She sat beside me on the couch; dog hair rubbed off on her sweater. Buster nudged our knees. She asked me how things were going, what was new. Generic questions. I set my scalding mug on the rickety table, wiped my hands on my jeans.

And I broke.

"There was this guy," I began, not meeting her eyes. I told her about Jack and me. That we'd met in Iraq. How, yes, he was married. How, no, it hadn't worked out.

I scrunched a paper towel to my face. It caught snot and tears, shame and pain. Before my mother could say a word in response, I let out a strangled yell, "I'm not you!"

She set her mug on the wooden floor, took my hand in hers.

"I'm sorry you've carried this with you," she said. "And I know you're not me." Then she shook her head. "Every decision you've ever made has been the opposite of what I've done."

I paused. By the time she was my age, my mom had been married, borne three children, and was contemplating divorce. Even when sitting on a pile of sandbags eight thousand miles away, I had never stopped to think how far I'd purposefully run.

I'd sprinted through MIT, the military, and most of a PhD program. *Only to screw up my whole life anyway*, I thought.

She hugged me hard; I breathed her scent. Her hair had the same brown fineness as mine.

"It's okay," she said. "You're my favorite daughter."

"Your *only* daughter," I sniffled, our longstanding exchange. Now I could exhale.

The tea mugs had gone cold. She hugged me good-bye and gently left me to my recovery.

• • •

That fall passed quickly. I ran every morning through browning leaves. Worked hard in the lab: booked midnight time on the electron beam writer, developed slides in the clean room around the clock. Disentangled my thoughts with the shrink. Nestled on sofas full of friends during Sunday football. Drank home-brewed beer with classmates in a professor's seaside backyard. Rolled gnocchi for potlucks. Even built the nerve to flirt with a cute guy in my Pilates class.

I also razored through a small fortress of self-help books. One sentence undid me: "We often re-create past situations in order to 'fix' them." The ethos of "leaving no one behind" didn't mean actively dragging someone backward, or letting them drag me. No matter how hard I had tried, reengaging with Jack would neither erase what we'd done on TQ nor repair what I'd endured as a kid.

No, it wouldn't.

So I agreed to lunch with Ryan, my Pilates classmate with close-cropped scruff and ocean blue eyes. Trained as an architect, he built furniture in his spare time. During his undergrad years, he'd participated in a cadet program similar to ROTC, but hadn't gone on to serve in the military. His long-distance girlfriend cooled my interest.

Still, we worked out together a few times as Christmas approached, clicking over postrun beers that turned into dinner that turned into late-night dog walks. He invited me to a movie at his apartment, where he'd designed and built every piece of furniture. After stuffed mushrooms and whiskey-spiked cocoa and ninety minutes of Wes Anderson, it became clear that we liked each other—and that he hadn't yet broken things off with his girlfriend. I left that night, honor intact. After a few more awkward interactions that winter, I told him he should handle his situation before we hung out again.

In February he met me in the cluttered basement lab where I worked alone. A blizzard whipped outside. As an atomic force microscope performed its quiet scan, Ryan stretched his legs and crossed one cowboy boot over another. He said he was in the midst of some hard conversations with his girlfriend. Though I appreciated his effort to update me, I drove home the point that I wouldn't see him again—not even for a run or a platonic dinner—until he was officially single.

Soon he was.

He was a maker—pizza from scratch, dresser drawers from salvaged poplar, custom shelves for my kitchen. We ran, hiked, and kayaked together; that summer we backpacked in Alaska. One afternoon at his apartment, he confessed his comfort music was James Taylor. I froze, mumbling something about Iraq. He smiled and took me into his arms. As the opening notes of *Handyman* sounded, I realized he owned a different album— not the soundtrack to war I remembered. And I had to admit there were songs in this world that I'd never heard before.

• • •

The winter I met Ryan, my cheap flip phone had shown a text from an unknown number: "Is this T?"

"Yes, who is this?" I'd written, though I already knew. It had been five months since Jack's last call.

His response took a day to arrive.

"This is Jack. I knew I wasn't going to have any more children, so that's why I didn't call. How are you?"

Five months of silence, and this was his opener? Was he fucking kidding?

And—a thought my friends had encouraged—*I can do better*. In those months, I'd also started writing. Dug out my black Iraq journal buried under green T-shirts and shorts. Found the secret text file kept on a scratched flash drive. Saved my deployment blog as a document, then password-protected it from the world. I was preparing the soil, the loam, for something to grow.

I waited a day and sent Jack one final text. "I'm doing great," I thumbed, walking Buster in clear morning light. "Good luck with everything."

Epilogue

Ten years to the day after leaving Iraq, I stepped off a train. It was a Thursday afternoon, and a cool breeze blew as the DC commuters debarked. I pulled down the sleeves of my black silk sweater, wishing I'd worn jeans instead of capris.

I was in Quantico to visit my old roommate Nell, her husband, and their three children. Nell was stationed there—the only one of us four old housemates still in the Marines. She'd been promoted to major the year before, and I found it hard to believe we were now the same age as Major Davis had been when I'd deployed. But I'd been to Nell's wedding, seen her pregnant, and watched her young family grow. She'd coached me through my breakup with Ryan, my brother Matt's deployments, and reconnections with my family. I couldn't wait to tell her more about the sweet engineer I'd been dating for over a year.

While scanning the platform for Nell's petite silhouette, I noticed a black Labrador. I still had a soft spot for Labs; Buster had been buried in my dad's backyard for three years. But this dog wore a blue vest. A service dog.

The crowd cleared. At the other end of the leash walked a tall, dark-haired man in khakis and polo, employee badge clipped to his belt.

He stepped closer, and I noticed his dimples. His green eyes focused on me.

"What are the chances?" Jack said.

"What *are* the chances?" I repeated. I didn't know what else to say.

He let me pet his dog, a gorgeous, calm girl. She lowered my spiking heart rate.

He blinked a few times, a tic I didn't recognize, and asked what I did for work. I'd defended my PhD and still worked in New York. He'd changed jobs in the last several years, to an impressive-sounding office gig.

Nell walked over and hugged me; gold oak-leaf insignia winked on her collar. When I introduced Jack, they shook hands, and I said politely that we should get going. I could barely stand straight, but shouldered my backpack and followed Nell to her van crammed with soccer balls and car seats.

"Who was that?" she asked, brushing granola crumbs from the upholstery.

In the parking lot, Jack climbed into a silver pickup, looked back once.

I raised a farewell arm.

Source Acknowledgments

Portions of this work first appeared as the following:

"Listening for Home," in *Retire the Colors*, ed. Dario DiBattista (Albany NY: Hudson-Whitman Excelsior College Press, 2016).

"Listening for Home," in *Invisible Veterans*, ed. Katie Hendricks Thomas and Kyleanne Hunter (Santa Barbara CA: Praeger, 2019).

"No One Left Behind," *Vassar Quarterly* 114, no. 3 (Fall 2015), https://vq.vassar.edu/issues/2015/03/web-extras/no-one-left-behind.html.

"Intrigue," *Consequence Magazine*, May 1, 2020, https://consequencemagazine.org/feature-of-the-month/intrigue/.

CAN'T HEAR

HEAR

KLANFER